THE

CHIPPENDALE PERIOD IN ENGLISH FURNITURE

Fig. 1.—Chippendale Furniture.

THE
CHIPPENDALE PERIOD
IN
ENGLISH FURNITURE

BY

K. WARREN CLOUSTON

WITH ILLUSTRATIONS BY THE AUTHOR

WEATHERVANE • BOOKS

First published in 1897 by Debenham & Freebody and
Edward Arnold

Library of Congress Catalog Card Number: 77-73595
This edition is published by Weathervane Books
a division of Imprint Society, Inc., distributed by Crown Publishers Inc.
by arrangement with EP Publishing Limited
a b c d e f g h

NOTE

HAVING, at various times, been requested by Messrs. Debenham and Freebody to give opinions upon pieces of old furniture, to catalogue collections purchased by them, and to make collections for them, I have now been asked by them to prepare a manual of the period of English furniture in which they are so greatly interested.

Contemporaneous literature on the subject of the Chippendale era is excessively scanty, and so many able writers have devoted themselves to saving what is left from oblivion, that most of the salient points have been already put before the public.

Though much time has been devoted to research, I have no wish to claim for the present volume the dignity of a history, but I feel no apology is required for placing before amateurs what I trust will be found to be a reliable handbook of this great English renaissance.

The illustrations have been taken from the original books of design, from national and private collections, as well as from specimens which Messrs. Debenham and Freebody have exhibited during the past few years.

K. W. C.

PUBLISHER'S NOTE

In order to issue this book in a modern printing style and at a reasonable price but without disturbing the original placement of illustrations, we have dropped the unnecessary blanks that once backed up the illustrations. The result is an unorthodox pagination, which we have not corrected so that the original index and table of contents will still be correct.

None of this interferes in any way with the usefulness and enjoyment of this classic furniture manual.

CONTENTS

LIST OF ILLUSTRATIONS

CHAPTER IV

CHAPTER V

CHAPTER VI

CHAPTER VII

CHAPTER VIII

I

INTRODUCTION

ART and convention are so wedded together that it is impossible wholly to dissever them. Where we find the best in art, we also find the best in convention. This would seem to lead to the conclusion that though art may be inherent in the race, it can only be called out to its fullest extent by the highest form of convention. As, therefore, convention must of necessity be a growth, gradually built up through innumerable stages, it would be altogether without parallel in the history of evolution if each of the forgotten steps did not influence the structure, and still more curious if we could not, where successive steps are left, trace the parentage of each new departure.

We hear a great deal about originality, and it is easy to talk glibly on the subject. It is, however, by no means so easy to give even an approximately correct definition of what originality really is. Where admissible influence ends and copying begins is a still more difficult problem. The one thing that seems to be certain is that the point is a variable one. There is a well-known proverb that one man may steal a horse out of a field, while another may not look over the hedge, and in nothing is it more true than in this same question of originality. William Shakespeare without William Shakespeare's genius would have been a thief pure and simple; as it is, he stands alone on the very apex and crown of originality. Lesser men have evolved plots strikingly new and treated them in a new manner, but the newness attained nothing beyond eccentricity, and eccentricity is no more originality than mannerism is style.

There is, of course, the possibility of a genius so transcendent that eccentricity and originality might be combined in his work, but the whole history of art is against the likelihood of such a combination.

The men to whom, after the test of centuries, we ascribe the honour of originality have all said or done things as old as the hills; and their claim to it consists, not in the novelty of the result, but in that absolutely indefinable impress of mind which is the criterion of all great work.

That this must be so is evident from the nature of things. Without education nothing great is possible, and education tends to make one see and assimilate only a small portion of the endless possibilities. Even the larger education which comes in after-life must necessarily be influenced by early teaching, and, in most cases, be limited to what is easily obtainable.

It is therefore essential, in order to understand, even superficially, the art of any time or country, to take into account the materials which lay to the artists' hands, and above all is this necessary in glancing at the art renaissance of the latter half of the eighteenth century in England.

By both birth and breeding the Anglo-Saxon was, before all things, a fighter, and our early history is one long tale of war and pillage. Art was left to women and to the Church, and it was the immense wealth and power of the Church that gave early England its one artistic advantage. The ecclesiastical architecture of the time, though lacking the gorgeous magnificence of what were then richer countries, is at least creditable and distinctive. The barons followed the lead of the churchmen, though their castles were not intended to be things of beauty, but strongholds. Moreover, the Church, in its architecture, gave no model for the conveniences of life. Indeed it must have mattered little to the old war-dogs, who, if not across the seas, were in the saddle most of their time, what might be the shape or design of their chairs or tables.

The Crusades gave the first impetus to domestic embellishment, and after them the numerous French wars brought models for our workmen. But, being won at the sword's point from a conquered people, the art that created them was despised as the attribute of an inferior race.

When, later in our history, the mercantile instincts of the nation began to develop, other causes militated against the formation of anything approaching to an English school in art of any kind. Some of the countries our merchants dealt with were much further advanced than ourselves, and whatever we exported in the way of manufactures could scarcely be artistic, while for home use beauty was of greatly minor importance to mere usefulness. So it came that, just as our soldiers carried home artistic spoils in earlier times, our merchants spread over the country the works of other lands, and our island became a sort of warehouse, so far as the more cultivated classes were concerned, for an infinity of works in different styles.

But order grew out of chaos, and in the sixteenth and seventeenth centuries we find oak furniture practically of native growth. There was evidence of Flemish influence certainly, but there was also a national distinctiveness both in the treatment of broad masses, and in the detail of design.

Oak lends itself to massiveness and grandeur of treatment, and these two qualities were admirably preserved by the designers of the time. It is more than a mere association of ideas which brings to our minds, even on the first glance at the boldness and majesty of their work, the " spacious times" to which they belonged. They have left us the very history and instincts of the race carved in our native wood. But nevertheless the style was doomed. Its splendour was too barbaric to suit the requirements of a time when refinement, if not effeminacy, had come to be the watchword. Oak had been carried as far as the inherent qualities of the wood allowed, and some other material was needed in which lightness and elegance could be more easily attained : something that would not necessarily suggest baronial halls and extempore barricades.

This need was supplied by the introduction of mahogany, and the workers of the Chippendale period seem to have instinctively grasped its capabilities. Flowing curves and delicately beautiful carving combined with high finish seem to have sprung into life almost at once. Greater lightness was afterwards achieved by Hepplewhite and Sheraton, but was the natural outcome of the revulsion against heaviness.

In painting, the result of the eighteenth-century art-wave was the formation of a school as entirely new as it is in the nature of things to be, but in the furniture of the same period the source from which the design sprang is more evident. This may be accounted for as much by the limitations of an art, conventional in its very essence, as by any lack of originality in the constructors. The rules and possibilities of decorative design, being much more limited than those of the painter's art, were naturally discovered sooner, and combination had to take the place of invention. If this is the case with decorative work generally, how much more is it so with the specialist who produces furniture only, and who is tied down first by his material, and secondly by his architect.

The historical presumption is that furniture of some sort or kind existed before even the rudest forms of architecture. The nomadic neolithic races, who bestowed such an infinity of time and pains on their most ordinary tools, had in all probability some light and portable articles which might be designated as furniture. When, therefore, man became dissatisfied with his bee-hive hut, and made his first attempts at architectural beauty, there must have been some existing forms of decoration which influenced the building. With a more fixed and permanent abode the relative positions of furniture and architecture changed places. Houses became a first and furniture a secondary consideration, for it was necessary that the movable objects should bear some relation to the interior fittings. Furniture was too closely allied to the decoration of the interior for the architect to be indifferent to it, so that he became the director of the craftsman in the important matters of proportion, style, and arrangement, and all good decoration not only emanated from architecture, but was an inherent part of it.

Earlier carvers had copied in wood the stonework of the exteriors, and the architect's designs for the lining of rooms must have given the keynote to furniture. The joiners who contracted for the wainscotting were very often employed to make the necessary tables and chairs, and would naturally repeat the ideas of the master builder. In the same way, the high-class cabinet and chair makers, who were called into existence by the increasing luxury of the times, were also compelled to follow, to a certain extent, what was already there; and the carved mahogany doors and chimney-pieces for which so many architects supply designs were carved by the very men who had begun to design the movable articles for themselves. So closely were the arts allied that not only did the architects of the eighteenth century design furniture, but some of the cabinet-makers laid claim to be architects. The painting of the walls, which followed the prevailing styles, was often copied upon the furniture; and the pattern, nay, even the colour, of Adam's plaster decoration was repeated on his cabinets and bookcases.

Through all the architectural work of the century there runs a strong vein of classicism. Occasional departures there were, as might have been expected, into Gothic, but in at least some of his work every man used the classic style. It was in the air, and had been for a century or more. That the great Inigo Jones used it would of itself have been sufficient to account for this; but when we remember the use that Sir Christopher Wren made of the opportunity that came to him for changing the face of London, it would have been little short of a miracle had the influence on succeeding architects been less than it was. In the Great Fire of 1666, 13,000 houses and 89 churches were destroyed; and Wren, by far the best architect of the time, must have influenced even what he did not build. His interior wood-work emulates the sumptuous grandeur of the Louis Quatorze period, and is undoubtedly responsible for the marked French taste which characterised most of his successors, and particularly influenced Grinling Gibbons, whose lifelike groups of fruit, flowers, and birds, founded the school to which Lock, Chippendale, and Johnson belonged.

Among those who kept up the classic feeling imparted to English architecture by Inigo Jones and Wren, were Sir John Vanbrugh, architect and playwright, who built Castle Howard and Blenheim; Hawksmoor, his friend and pupil; and Gibbs, a Scottish architect and antiquary, to whom we owe the Radcliffe Library at Oxford, and the church of St. Martin-in-the-Fields. The latter followed closely in Wren's footsteps; indeed it was to him that the task of finishing St. Clement Danes in the Strand was entrusted when the death of Wren left it incomplete. He published his *Book of Architecture* in 1728, in which the designs for mantel-pieces are evidently the foundation of those of more than one of his successors, while his profuse adaptation of urns and stone globes to both the exterior and interior of domestic buildings was also closely copied.

Among those who strove to keep up the style of Inigo Jones are Colin Campbell, Thomas Archer, and William Kent. The work Campbell commenced under the title of *Vitruvius Britannicus* was afterwards added to by other architects, but his long list of the principal houses then lately erected in England makes us acquainted with the works and names of men of whom we should never else have heard. He, as well as the other architects, helped to build the many great manorial mansions throughout the country in the Italian style which Inigo Jones had imbibed when he was sent abroad by the Earl of Pembroke.

Kent was another architect of about the same calibre, but the assistance and patronage of the gifted Earl of Burlington had helped him to a more extended popularity, though from the latter's modesty it is difficult to know how much should be credited to his patron and how much to himself. Together they re-fronted Burlington House and the Treasury Buildings at Whitehall, but Kent constructed the Horse Guards alone. Combining the profession of landscape gardener with those of allegorical painter, architect, and decorative authority, he was employed in the gardens at Carlton House, Claremont, and Chiswick, much as Sir William Chambers afterwards was at Kew. In this he for once forsook his artificiality, and succeeded so well in the natural style as to earn from

FIG. 2.—STONE MANTELPIECE, from James Gibbs' "Book of Architecture," 1728.

Horace Walpole the title of "Father of Modern Gardening." To us he is chiefly interesting on account of his furniture designs, which, though far from perfect, heralded the approach of the day when architecture and furniture designing actually joined hands. To show how much he was esteemed in his own time, notwithstanding much adverse criticism, it may be mentioned that Chambers in his work on Kew Gardens, thirty years later, gives a long list of gilded decorations and furniture in the Palace "designed by the late ingenious Mr. Kent." His authority dominated public taste, and he was referred to on all such matters as frames, glasses, tables, chairs, cradles, "birthday gowns," and even barges.

His illustrated works on architectural ornament show how books were beginning to be published as a guide to style. As early as 1727 he published two folio volumes of Inigo Jones's works, with several by the Earl of Burlington, and some chimney-pieces and sections of rooms by himself, as well as a few by Palladio. In 1744 Kent again put forth examples of his great model's work with some of his own designs to secure more consideration for the latter, and also to prove from whence he derived his inspiration. His own contributions of "candlesticks for the

FIG. 3.—CHIMNEY-PIECE for Lord Pembroke's house at Wilton. By Inigo Jones. From Designs by Inigo Jones and Kent, 1744.

King, a section of Merlin's Cave in the Royal Gardens at Richmond, a mantel-piece of hunting scenes for the Prince of Wales, a slab table for Lord Orford, two vases with pedestals for Mr. Pope, a Gothic screen for Gloucester Cathedral," and numerous gold and silver standishes, cups, and dish-covers, give a slight idea of the comprehensive range of his subjects, but not of his weak designs.

In a description (1760) Kent gives us of Houghton Hall, constructed for Sir Robert Walpole by Ripley from Campbell's original designs, we have a very forcible picture of both the varied style and magnificent decoration then existing in some of the houses of the higher nobility.

The drawing-room was hung with "caffoy," the salon with crimson flowered velvet, and Kent himself painted the ceilings and designed the

FIG. 4.—CHIMNEY-PIECE in the Hall of Sir Robert Walpole's house at Houghton.   William Kent.

black and gold chimney-piece, though Horace Walpole in his *Anecdotes of Painting* rather ill-naturedly records that his father " would not permit him to paint in colours, but restrained him to chiaroscuro." In the "common parlour" was some "fine pear-tree carving by Gibbons," while another had the walls entirely lined with marble. The bed-chambers were heavy with gold-lined velvet, tapestry, or needlework hangings, and some of the smaller rooms were wainscotted with mahogany, with an alcove of the same wood for the bed.

Architects were not alone at this time in their influence on furniture design. It is worthy of note that Hogarth, both as painter and caricaturist, was a distinct factor in the adoption of a more flowing line. Though painting Kent's heavily classic interiors, he used his satire to throw ridicule on them and their author's weakness and incompetency. The five orders of architecture came in for a share of his mockery, and in his *Analysis of Beauty* he introduced cabriole legs by way of illustration. So captivated was he by the serpentine line that he regarded it as the denominator of all beauty, and said: "There is scarce a room in any house whatever where one does not see the waving line employed in some way or other. How inelegant would the shape of our movables be without it! How very plain and unornamental the mouldings of cornices and chimney-pieces without the variety introduced by the *ogee* member, which is entirely composed of waving lines!" Following this out, and choosing wherever possible furniture which carried out the flowing line he so industriously preached, he did much to popularise curved form and to prepare the way for the success of Chippendale and the later schools.

Previous to this time there had been but few attempts at literature relating to interior decoration. Doors and chimney-pieces indeed were included in some of the architectual works, but W. Jones was the first to bring out an illustrated book bearing more directly on furniture. His *Gentlemen's or Builders' Companion* (1739) is of modest size and scope, with only a small quantity of plates, the greater number being intended to be carried out in stone. Jones describes himself as an architect, and, though one of small repute, gives good but heavy designs for temples, doors and gateways, railings, and gate-piers, much in the style of his more famous predecessors. His designs for domestic architecture are of the same classic nature as his exterior decoration. The chimney-pieces with structural overmantels have pictures and square mirrors competing for the place of honour; but he, like Gibbs and Kent, also gives designs for the "lower part of chimney-pieces in stone or wood," as unfortunately these hitherto close friends were beginning to part company. Yet so quickly did changes come about that hardly twenty years sufficed to change the ponderous character of these chimney-pieces into the light, fanciful productions of Chippendale and Johnson.

FIG. 5.—CHIMNEY-PIECE FOR A GRAND APARTMENT. William Jones.

Mirrors and slab tables are the only furniture introduced. The mirrors resemble those in his overmantels, and are square in shape, plain and severe, but they indicate how the interrupted arch and swan-necked pediments, hitherto confined to stone, were beginning to be introduced

into furniture.   The designs for slab tables show elaborate carving, with
a massive shell in the centre, and heavy festoons of flowers from one side
to the other, while some are supported by caryatides surrounded with
foliage and scrollwork.   Jones lays little claim to merit, and does not
seem to have received much recognition, though his book is quite as
interesting as that which Kent issued in 1744.

About the middle of the century Sir Robert Taylor and James Paine
divided the profession of architecture between them, till the Adam brothers

FIG. 6.—SQUARE MIRROR.   William Jones.

entered the lists and distinguished themselves by the superiority of their
taste and the greater delicacy of their decoration.   Meanwhile Chambers,
under royal patronage, was gradually making his way to a foremost position,
and displayed his talents in Somerset House, the greatest architectural work
of the reign of George the Third.   Though one of the most correct and
painstaking architects of his century, he was not employed on any churches
of importance, nor did he receive the great patronage from the nobility which
fell to the Adams' share.   He adapted to English buildings the principles
of art gathered from the works of Michael Angelo, Vignola, Palladio, and
Bernini, and indulged his fondness for Chinese and Turkish architecture in

the gardens placed in his hands.   Robert Adam, who had filled his portfolio
with innumerable drawings and sketches from the inexhaustible mines of
Italy and Greece, acquired a reputation for classical knowledge which his
buildings hardly justified, as in this respect they were inferior to those of
Chambers.   Like him, Adam brought his knowledge and skill to bear on
interior decoration, and notwithstanding his delicate but too lace-like forms,

FIG. 7.—SLAB TABLE.   William Jones.

laid the foundation of even a more lasting school.   The few ornamental
articles for household use which Chambers actually constructed grew under
Adam into the entire fittings of a room, and caused the designing of useful
articles to take a much higher stand than it had previously attained.

The Gothic vein which ran through eighteenth - century design had
very little of the spirit or merit of the original.   Though the works
which Wren (St. Michael's, Cornhill, and St. Dunstan's-in-the-East) and

Hawksmoor (All Saints, Oxford) had erected in that style showed appreciation of the grander forms, with contempt for the details, the followers of the Gothic revival in the eighteenth century carried out the minutiæ with more or less indifference to the general features. The credit, if credit there be, of first bringing about a Gothic revival ought certainly to be given to Horace Walpole, better known under that name than as Earl of Orford. His "whole life," we are told, "was spent in snatching from time the few remaining specimens of classic ages, the treasures of Gothic halls and cathedrals, and antiquities of the Middle Ages." In the house commenced at Strawberry Hill in 1753 he endeavoured to combine details borrowed from the fourteenth and fifteenth centuries with the residence of a country gentleman of the eighteenth. The carvings in stone and marble were supposed to be actual representations of the details of York Minster and many equally celebrated buildings, and the example set here was copied in ecclesiastical architecture as well as in domestic buildings throughout the country. Castles were built with nicked parapets and windows in the form of a cross with round terminations at the end. Most architects were betrayed into a little deviation towards Gothic. Robert Adam, who had assisted with some of the interior details of Strawberry Hill, built Colzean Castle and more of the same class, besides designing in "Georgian Gothic" for Alnwick Castle and other houses.

Wyatt, whose restorations of Lincoln, Salisbury, and other cathedrals earned him a doubtful title to fame, was one of the greatest exponents of the Gothic school. His work had originally been in the classic style, and his drawings of fine rosetted ceilings, now in the South Kensington Museum, prove him a talented designer. Domestic Gothic smouldered through all the later years of the century till it burst into renewed life in the building of the short-lived Fonthill Abbey, in which Wyatt challenged comparison with Strawberry Hill.

Just in the same way Gothic flickered through the woodwork, shooting up every here and there in furniture design; and curious bookcases, tables, and chairs were made to agree with the taste for accurate detail. This was only one of the many influences which worked on Chippendale and his followers, and we can trace the Gothic feeling in his work as surely as the many other elements which went to make up the perfect whole. All schools were requisitioned by him, though Gothic may not have been so strong as that of other influences which formed what we know as the Chippendale style.

The tendency to Grecian architecture, fostered by the Dilettanti Society, and greatly advanced by the publication of Stuart's *Antiquities of Athens*, became popular in the next epoch, greatly influencing the later work of Sheraton, and the early designers of the present century.

Having traced the influence of architecture on the eighteenth-century school, it may be well to refer to the sources which lay ready to the designers' hands, and from which many of their more immediate ideas were taken. Before this era, the necessity for turning to other nations more advanced than ourselves in domestic arts led to skilled architects, artists, and craftsmen being brought from Italy, France, and Flanders, to satisfy the taste for beauty which our nation had developed, but which our backward manufacturers were unable to supply. Increased trade and more luxurious habits led the wealthier classes to look on travel as a necessary part of education, and also sent traders abroad to purchase not only decorative objects, but books of designs. Publications on ornament had appeared in France as early as 1550, especially works bearing immediately on carving; for, as in our own country the demand for mirror-frames, chimney-pieces, and overmantels, called skilled carvers into being, so abroad this class of work led the van in decorative improvement. These new books of design were continuously appearing; so that even if our designers did not travel, they had the works of their contemporaries brought to their doors.

In the reign of the earlier Georges there existed a great mania for everything French, and, though not so palpable later, this continued throughout the century. Nevertheless, a school more insular in taste was springing up, and was fostered by the growing feeling of the country and the desire to evince loyalty to the king, foreign though he was, and to show no leaning to the " king over the water."

The Chippendale school, for the first time in our history, caused the eyes of other countries to be turned to us as a centre of furniture design. The style was not, and could not have been, of native growth, but was, like ourselves, a mixture of every race and country ; and, just as we are none the less English for our mixture of bloods, so is Chippendale's furniture also English although he adopted various foreign *motifs* in its design. He had probably less idea of forming a school than Adam or many of his successors, still his earnest endeavours to improve English design led to the foundation of a deeper and more national movement than anything of which he could possibly have dreamt. The position of design became reversed, for when enough time had elapsed to allow the style to become properly formed, his books and furniture were taken over the seas to be copied by other countries. National pride and the isolation induced by our foreign wars also caused a demand for purely English manufactures, and though the designers owed much to foreign inventions, still they added to them a practical sobriety eminently characteristic of the English race. Even Sheraton, as ready to draw on foreign sources as any of his brother craftsmen, kept up the traditions of our greatness, and, competing with his foreign rivals more successfully than he was himself aware of, became a power in the world of design.

II

SIR WILLIAM CHAMBERS

FEW men have left a greater mark on the art productions of their time than Sir William Chambers. Just as Reynolds's spirit is everywhere manifest in English eighteenth-century painting, so both the architecture and the cabinet-making of the period were greatly indebted to Chambers. He did not, indeed, possess the originality of the great master, who, by the work of his own brush, formed a school which bore little or no resemblance to anything that went before it. Chambers's forte lay not in producing anything strikingly new, but in adapting what had gone before to his own purposes; and though we may regret that his style was so essentially un-English, we cannot fail to admit the exquisite taste which pervades his use of the foreign material with which he worked. In the designs of Chippendale the classicism is somewhat toned down, and shows a purer English spirit, and for a time it seemed as if furniture were to follow a slightly different line from architecture. But Chambers had set the ball rolling, and Adam, who began where he left off, out-heroded Herod in his slaughter of anything and everything of purely English birth in both arts.

It is a little curious that Scotland, at that time far behind the sister country in painting, should have produced both Chambers and Adam, by far the greatest architects of their time. The former, though born in Sweden in 1726, was the scion of an old Scotch family. His grandfather, who settled there, supplied the armies of Charles XII. with money and stores, and suffered greatly by the base coin he received in return. On his death, the son, William's father, remained in the country in order to prosecute his claims, but in 1728 returned to England, and settled on an estate near Ripon, where Sir William Chambers was educated.

Chambers had a great love of the sea, and, as a mere lad, made several

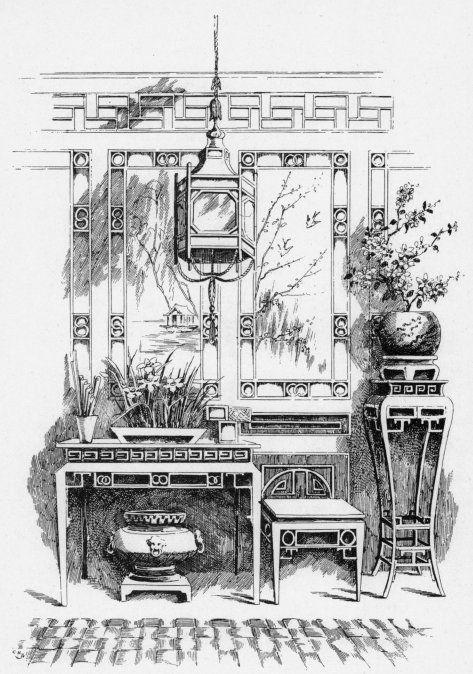

FIG. 8.—A CHINESE ROOM.   From Sir William Chambers's "Book of Chinese Buildings, Furniture, etc."

voyages in the capacity of supercargo to the Swedish East India Company. During one of these journeys he visited Canton, and remained there a considerable time to study the peculiar habits, costumes, and buildings of the Chinese. These made so great an impression upon him that he took careful sketches and notes, not only of the buildings and furniture, but of the Chinese taste in gardening, which he made full use of afterwards.

FIG. 9.—CHINESE TABLE.   From Sir William Chambers's Book.

In 1757 he embodied the result of his travels in a large folio, embellished with engravings by Rooker, Fourdrinier, Grignon, and Paul Sandby. This was also published in French under the title of *Edifices, Meubles, Habits, Machines, et Utensiles des Chinois*. This book, and its author's influence, greatly increased the rage for the Chinese style in this country, and laid the foundation for a taste which has never been wholly eradicated; but it is only fair to Chambers to say that, though he was publishing a book on Chinese architecture, he did not wish it to be suspected that his intention was to "promote a taste so much inferior to the antique."

He looked on Chinese buildings as "toys in architecture, and as toys are sometimes, on account of their oddity, prettiness, or neatness of workmanship, admitted into the cabinets of the curious, so may Chinese buildings be sometimes allowed a place among compositions of a nobler kind." He adds that, "generally speaking, Chinese architecture does not suit European purposes; yet in extensive parks and gardens, or in large palaces, containing a numerous series of apartments, I do not see the impropriety of finishing some of the inferior ones in Chinese taste"; so he adds to his designs "furniture taken from such models as appeared to me most beautiful and reasonable. Some are pretty, and may be useful to our cabinet-makers."

Though Chippendale's book was published three years before this, it is quite possible that the original drawings made by Chambers in China may have influenced him in preparing the *Gentleman and Cabinet-maker's Director*. Chippendale's work is so much more correct than what went before him in this style, that the likelihood of his having access to better material is very great. This view would fall in with the generally received idea that Chambers was the real originator of the Chinese style, which, however, is not borne out by the date of publication.

After illustrating the pagodas, temples, and people, Chambers gives a description of a Chinese room. "The side-walls are matted about three or four feet upwards from the pavement, the rest being covered with white, crimson, or gilt paper; and instead of pictures they hang on them long pieces of satin or paper, stretched on frames, and painted in imitation of marble or bamboo, on which are written moral sentences or proverbs. Sometimes they hang a very large sheet of thick paper, covered with antique Chinese paintings, enclosed in panels of different figures."

"The movables in the saloon consist of chairs, stools, and tables, made sometimes of rosewood, ebony, or lacquered work, and sometimes of bamboo only, which is cheap, and nevertheless very neat. When the movables are of wood, the seats of the stools are often of marble or porcelain, which, though hard to sit on, are far from unpleasant in a climate where the summer heats are so excessive. In the corners of the rooms are stands four or five feet high, on which they set plates of citrons and other fragrant fruits, or branches of coral in vases of porcelain, and glass globes containing goldfish, together with a certain weed somewhat resembling fennel; on such tables as are intended for ornament only they also place little landscapes, composed of rocks, shrubs, and a kind of lily that grows among pebbles covered with water. . . . But among the principal ornaments of these rooms are the lanterns, of which there are generally four suspended from the ceiling by silken cords."

Chambers seems to have had very little idea of the effect this book would have; in fact, he rather apologises for its appearance. His friends, he tells us, tried to dissuade him from publishing his Chinese designs, lest it should hurt his reputation as an architect; but he says that he himself is unable

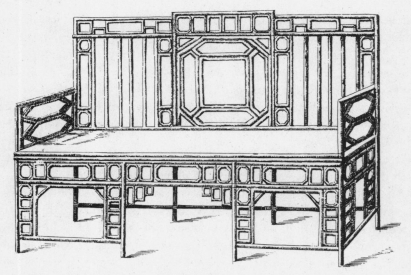

FIG. 10.—CHINESE SEAT. From Sir William Chambers's "Book of Chinese Buildings, etc."

to see why, as a traveller, he should not give an account of what he had seen worthy of notice. If, therefore, the Chinese taste brought in by other and smaller men died, he was not committed to anything; whereas, if his book and Chippendale's *Director* (then lately published) brought the style into sufficient notice, he would reap considerable advantage as an architect from its publication. This indeed was exactly what happened. His book served to set the hall-mark of authority on the fashion, which, his disclaimer notwithstanding, has ever since been more connected with his name than with any other. As an older man there is no trace of timidity in his Chinese publications. The style had taken root, and he, as a recognised authority, could say what he pleased without fear or favour.

Shortly after his voyages, and long before the publication of this book, when he was about eighteen, Chambers abandoned commercial pursuits, and gave himself up wholly to the study of architecture. It was only natural that, living at a time when the "grand tour" was part of a gentleman's education, Chambers should go abroad to study. Sir Joshua Reynolds himself was at that very time on the Continent, but Sir Joshua had already formed his style, and Italian influence plays

FIG. 11.—CHINESE FURNITURE.
From Sir William Chambers's Book.

FIG. 12.—"GUERIDON" WITH VASE
AND CORAL SPRAY. From Sir
William Chambers's Book.

but a small part in his creations. Chambers, on the other hand, went as a student pure and simple, and either had not arrived at that stage where it is possible to benefit from a style without of necessity adopting it, or did not possess the originality to use without appearing to copy. Foreign influence is not always for good. In Sir Joshua's works it can only be traced (except in a few isolated instances) by greater breadth of view; to Wilkie, on the other hand, it did irretrievable harm. What Chambers and Adam might have been without the training they gave themselves in classic architecture it is impossible to say, but it is probable that, in both cases, correct taste was formed at the expense of originality.

The chief point, however, is that the two greatest architects of the latter half of the eighteenth century not only imbibed new tastes and aims from Continental study, but, of necessity, grafted these tastes and aims on to English furniture.

When Chambers returned to England in 1755, he was accompanied by Wilton and Cipriani, afterwards so well known as an artist and decorator. He also brought Italian sculptors to carve the marble mantelpieces he introduced into English houses. These were made from his own designs, and the ornament of figures, scrolls, and foliage was free in

FIG. 13.—MARBLE MANTELPIECE.   Designed by Sir William Chambers.

character. Strange to say, these mantelpieces, designed and made by an architect, were yet the means of taking away this important part of interior decoration from the hands of the architects altogether, and causing it to become quite a separate production, made and sold along with the grates. In former times it had been an integrant portion of the room, reaching from floor to ceiling, balanced and made part of the wall by having its main lines carried round in panelling and enriched friezes. It was the keynote of decoration, and the master builder of the time grew fanciful, and exerted his utmost skill upon its carving and quaint imagery, centralising the whole ornament of the room around this household shrine.

Mantelpieces had gradually come down in height, though still retaining much of their fine proportion and classic design. Many causes had contributed to this, the chief being the disuse of wood panelling, and the preference given to hangings of damask, foreign leather, and wall-paper. In the reigns of Queen Anne and the "Little Dutchman" the custom of panelling was partially kept up, but the lining was only white painted deal, after the fashion in Holland. At this time the upper part of the chimney-piece was still retained, but only reached about half-way up the wall. Gibbs, Kent, and Ware kept the superstructure as much as they could, but Sir William Chambers dealt it the most crushing blow it had yet received by copying the later French and Italian styles, and giving minute detail more consideration than fine proportion. He discarded the upper part altogether, and helped to make "continued chimney-pieces" things of the past. His elegant marble mantelpieces in low relief may have assisted the growing taste for fine decoration, but they led to the chimney-piece being made in large quantities by manufacturers, and inserted at the purchaser's discretion, without any reference to the style of the room. In his *Treatise on Civil Architecture* he remarks that "England is at present possessed of many able sculptors, whose chief employment being to execute marble chimney-pieces, now happily in vogue, it may be said that in this particular we surpass all others in taste of design and goodness of workmanship."

The taste for Italian design, with its minute attention to detail, which he had imbibed so thoroughly, blinded him to the fact that these much-lauded mantelpieces were but a poor substitute for the former boldness of the purer classic style; but, the change once made, classic severity was still more departed from, and the vagaries of the Louis Quinze period, Chinese fancies, or pointed Gothic were introduced to suit the whim of the moment. Further innovations crept in later, and chimney-piece decoration was adapted to suit each particular style. Though Chambers had a large share in bringing about these innovations, he was not so ready to encourage the jasper chimney ornaments which Wedgwood was beginning to make, and seemed to have altogether failed to appreciate their delicate beauty. This may have been partly because they might have interfered with the sale of his own wares, which his father-in-law, Wilton, disposed of so freely. Had Chambers chosen, he could have done much to bring them into notice; for he had often full liberty given him, as in the case of Lord Melbourne's house, to introduce any simple, yet striking, style of decoration.

In 1759 Chambers published his well-known treatise on *The Decorative Part of Civil Architecture*, which reached a second edition in 1769, and a third in 1791. Despite his depreciation of Greek architecture, this book will always take a first place as a text-book on classicism, and is exceedingly valuable to architectural students.

About this date Chambers was appointed to teach drawing to the young Prince of Wales, afterwards George the Third. This was sufficient to ensure royal favour for the rest of his life; for, on coming to the throne, his royal patron appointed him his architect. His success, however, was not merely the result of patronage, his own ability and merits being quite sufficient to ensure his reputation.

When Augusta, Dowager Princess of Wales, was seeking an architect to adorn the gardens of her villa or palace at Kew, Mr. Chambers (for he was not yet Sir William) received the commission. This gave him the opportunity of indulging his taste for both classic and Chinese architecture, and he erected several semi-Roman temples, besides mosques and summer-houses, which were derided as "unmeaning falballas of Turkish and Chinese chequer-work." The well-known Pagoda was the most important of the oriental buildings. Whatever may be thought of these nowadays, they certainly gave great satisfaction at the time, and Chambers celebrated them in 1763 in a volume to which he contributed the architectural designs, Cipriani the figures, and Kirby, T. Sandby, and Marlow the views.

That this style was not wholly new to England is proved by Chambers mentioning in this work that a Chinese octagon in these gardens, built by Goupy a good many years before, had the walls and ceilings painted with gilt ornaments and scenes from the life of Confucius.

Royalty having set the fashion, the country loyally followed, and Chinese architecture became the rage. Not only were summer-houses and other buildings erected in Chinese form, but we find it mixed up with all the ornament of the period. Room walls were covered with scenes of Chinese life, either in painted panels or on paper, showing bridges and boats, or Chinamen ascending impossible staircases. Every article in the room was framed in accordance, so real Chinese lacquer and its English imitation advanced still further into favour. More widely spread than the unmistakable rage for Japanese within our recollection, the Chinese mania left its mark deeply impressed on the productions of the century. All the furniture catalogues published about this time were marked by its influence. Chippendale's and Johnson's pagodas, bells, mandarins, and dragons were some of the early examples of this craze in furniture, while Mayhew, Ince, and Manwaring exemplify its worst features. Even Lock, who followed the classic in his other work, was led away by this phase of popular fashion.

As a rule, the square shape and rectilinear form of ornament was mostly

FIG. 14.—CHINESE CHAIR IN ROUNDED WOOD, TO IMITATE BAMBOO.

copied ; but chairs of rounded wood were sometimes made from Chambers's drawings, and Sheraton, in his *Cabinet Dictionary*, mentions that they were " of turned beech, or painted to match the colours of the reed or cane."

The side of a room, reproduced from Chambers's book, will give some idea of the Chinese style carried out in its entirety, as he intended it to be. That his imitators mixed it up without meaning is no reason why the style itself should be condemned. Even Chippendale made a sort of *olla podrida* of Chinese, Gothic, and Flamboyant French ; while Sheraton, towards the end of the century, gives two designs of the Prince of Wales's

Chinese drawing-room, showing ultra-Chinese character on the walls and general decoration, while the chairs are entirely after his own semi-French designs.

It was not, however, the mere suggestion of an ephemeral taste that caused Chambers to rank among the pioneers of the best known period of eighteenth-century furniture. His influence is apparent in the work of almost all the designers who succeeded him. In Chippendale's book, the cabinets and bookcases are distinctly reminiscent of Chambers, and the same is true, in a greater degree, of the work of most of the later cabinet-makers.

The position of Royal Architect and Comptroller of the Royal Works brought him into communication with all the first men of the day, and his own artistic and literary talent enabled him to number Reynolds, Johnson, Goldsmith, and Garrick among his personal friends. His opinion was consulted on all occasions; he was " the oracle of taste," so that it is probable, apart from his own absolute work, he had much to do with originating a great deal of the style which now goes under the name of " Chippendale." He was, as has been said, in a position to introduce his ideas into the houses he designed, and the interest he took in the ordinary articles of household furniture must have had great influence on Adam and other architects. Cosmopolitan in his views, and full of learning and culture, he endeavoured to bring into vogue whatever he considered best and finest, and helped to sow the seed which was afterwards to produce such great results in the history of English design.

The year 1768 saw the inauguration of the Royal Academy of Arts, with Reynolds as president and Chambers as treasurer and member. Soon after this he was knighted by George the Third, and about the same time the King of Sweden, in return for some drawings, made the *amende honorable* for wrongs done to his family, by bestowing on him the order of the Polar Star. Chambers brought much ridicule upon himself by his *Dissertation on Oriental Gardening* (1772), for which the absurd depreciation of nature in the most bombastic style, and the ridiculous designs of the Emperor of China's Gardens, were quite sufficient to account. His endeavour to prove the superiority of the Chinese system of landscape gardening over that practised in Europe is little short of laughable. But so great was his name that the book, which had vignettes by Bartolozzi, actually ran into a second edition in twelve months.

What is generally considered to be Sir William's masterpiece dates from 1775, in which year the erection of Somerset House was placed in his hands. The whole of this extensive building was from his own designs ; and though opinions differ greatly as to the value of the work, it is generally admitted that the terrace is boldly conceived, the interiors fine, and the staircases masterpieces. Though so much good detail abounds, many consider it deficient in the art of architectural massing ; he was, moreover, severely and justly criticised for demolishing the old façade facing the river, which had been constructed by Inigo Jones.

Although not nearly so much patronised by the nobility as the Adams, he designed mansions for Earl Gower at Whitehall, for Lord Melbourne in Piccadilly, Charlemont House, Dublin, Wilton House for Earl Pembroke, a villa at Roehampton for the Earl of Bessborough, Duddingston House, near Edinburgh, for Lord Abercorn, and additions and alterations in the Gothic style to Milton Abbey, near Dorchester. He passed into retirement some years before his death, but it is satisfactory to know that on his decease in 1796 he received the honour of burial in Westminster Abbey.

To Sir William Chambers we owe a more flowing design, with charmingly delicate carving of flowers, plants, and other objects adapted to architectural ornament. The trouble he took to teach the decorative artists and artificers who were employed by him effected an enormous improvement in the unmeaning forms which had been common in the previous century, and the Royal State coach which he designed and Cipriani painted still remains as an evidence of his versatile skill. His original drawings for interior decoration, now in the South Kensington Museum, are full of the ideas gleaned in his varied travels, skilfully adapted to suit English interiors. One of the most noticeable features is the colouring. Both the ceiling and mural decorations are of the highest order, while the execution throughout is thorough and artistic, especially as regards the frescoes and recess ornaments. The wreaths, festoons, vases, and columns in some of these designs are the basis of a great deal of the later work of the century, while Sheraton and Hepplewhite undoubtedly found forms for painting and inlaying amongst the musical trophies and cherub groups.

FIG. 15.—A CHIPPENDALE ROOM.

III

THOMAS CHIPPENDALE

CONTEMPORANEOUS opinion of the work of any artist is apt to be fallacious, and in few instances where the artist has met with any success at all, is this more evident than in the case of Thomas Chippendale. Very little notice is taken either of him or his work in the literature or letters of the period, and where he is mentioned at all, it is generally in depreciatory terms. Even Sheraton, who owed his very existence to the demand which Chippendale had greatly called into being, is no exception. The master cabinet-maker could barely have been more than cold in his grave when he damns him with faint praise and consigns his work to oblivion as antiquated.

Time has avenged Thomas Chippendale, and he now holds a place unique in the annals of furniture. When we speak of any of the other styles, we name them after the reigning monarch of the period. We talk of the Elizabethan, Jacobean, Queen Anne, Louis Quatorze, or Louis Quinze periods, without once dreaming of any injustice to the designers; but when we speak of that great period of English furniture design which extended from the middle to the end of the eighteenth century, we for once forget crowned heads, and call the era by the name of a man who kept a shop in St. Martin's Lane.

Heredity, as well as individual capacity, had a great deal to do with Chippendale's success. A talent for carving was inherent in his family, his father having made a name among the upper classes in London for his carved mirrors and picture frames. The Chippendale who is famous all the world over was born in Worcestershire, but beyond that nothing is known of his personal history. What little information we have is gleaned almost entirely from the pages of his book. The dates of his birth and death are lost, and the name of " Thomas Chippendale, Upholsterer," which appeared in Sheraton's *Cabinet Dictionary* among " a List of most of the

Master Cabinet-makers, Upholsterers, and Chairmakers in and about London in 1803," was, in all likelihood, that of his son; for George Smith, Upholsterer to His Majesty at the beginning of this century (writing in 1826), alludes to the author of the *Director* as the "elder Mr. Chippendale," and fixes the approximate date of the son's death by stating that "Mr. Thomas Chippendale (lately deceased), though possessing a great degree of taste and ability as a draughtsman and designer, was known only to a few."

The dwelling-place as well as the shop of the Chippendale family was situated in St. Martin's Lane, at that time a fashionable and artistic quarter. There Hogarth had studied in Sir James Thornhill's studio, and there the Academy of Arts was born. The first members must often have strolled in to see the Court Upholsterer and talk over his designs; who knows but Sir Joshua, then only Mr. Reynolds may not have had a hand in helping the Master Cabinet-maker to his wonderful power of spacing, a quality Sir Joshua exhibited so largely in his pictures. For art and cabinet-making went hand in hand. We have seen how the first treasurer of the Academy was an art decorator as well as an architect, and many of the earlier members painted groups and panels for furniture both on mahogany and satin-wood.

Chippendale's first known plates are dated 1753, and the *Gentleman and Cabinet-maker's Director* came out in 1754, followed by a second edition in 1759, and a third in 1762; this rapid publication showing the increased interest which was being taken in cabinet-making generally.

Indeed it is curious that at only one short period of our literary history was it possible for furniture-makers to publish illustrated catalogues on anything like a commercial basis. Before Chippendale's day there had not been enough interest taken in the subject, and in our own time the public have been led to expect such productions gratis. But the fact remains that it was possible for Chippendale to publish a volume costing £3 : 13 : 6, the price at which the limited number of copies of the *Gentleman and Cabinet-maker's Director* was sold, and yet have it pass into several editions in a short time.

Though this was the first book of any great moment, and the ground-work for most of the succeeding illustrated catalogues, still, as we have seen, there had been a few attempts at such literature previously, but not of such importance as to call much attention to themselves or their authors.

Chippendale's production was of folio size, with one hundred and sixty copperplates. The fancy for bombastic dedications, which called forth Hogarth's satire, was in full vigour, so he inscribes the first edition to Prince William Henry, and another to the Earl of Northumberland, to whom he alludes in grandiloquent terms as having " an intimate acquaintance with all those arts and sciences that tend to perfect and adorn life." No work of the kind was ever attempted without a list of subscribers, and Chippendale himself remarks that the names which he secured belong to all degrees of life, from the Duke of Northumberland to William Frank, bricklayer. The list includes large numbers of men following the same trade as Chippendale, not only in London, but all over the country, though none of them have been remembered save William Ince and his partner Mayhew. Chippendale tells us that he has been encouraged to carry out the work " by persons of distinction and taste, who have regretted that an art capable of so much perfection and refinement should be executed with so little propriety and elegance." He leaves the reader to determine how much his sheets of designs will do to remove this just complaint, but feels that his pencil has but faintly copied out the images his fancy suggested. His friends in the Academy had evidently been comforting him over this, for he says he has " been told that all masters of every other art have laboured under the same difficulty."

Chippendale prepares to repay the criticisms which will be levelled at his work, by contempt, and "leaves the critics to convince the world they have neither the good nature to commend, the judgment to correct, nor the skill to execute what they find fault with." Some severe remarks had undoubtedly been launched at his furniture already, for he is careful to state that he gives no designs but what any skilful workman can execute, though some of his profession have been diligent enough to represent them as so many specious drawings, impossible to be carried out by any mechanic whatever. Chippendale attributes these aspersions to malice, ignorance, or inability, and assures those who honour him with their commands that he can improve upon every design in the execution of it.

In prefixing a short explanation of the never-to-be-forgotten five orders, Chippendale acknowledges his indebtedness to architecture by saying : " Of all the arts which are either improved or ornamented by it, that of cabinet-making is not only the most useful and ornamental, but capable of receiving as great assistance from it as any whatever." The pedantically exact drawings of the five orders were probably due to the architectural knowledge of his friend and engraver Darly. They appear to be introduced merely to give a learned air to the work. At the time he wrote, knowledge of these classic styles was regarded as the foundation of all art education, so it naturally looked well to hold them up as models. Chippendale, though moulding the proportions and general form of his cabinets and bookcases on these lines, never attempted to go any nearer; indeed he has even been

FIG. 16.—PARLOUR CHAIR. Chippendale.

accused of a lack of architectural feeling. But we must remember that there were two Chippendales—Chippendale the theorist, and Chippendale the worker. The theorist gives us a disquisition on the five orders of architecture; the worker, having sacrificed to these fashionable gods, goes his way, in supreme indifference of rule, and gives full scope to his genius for composition.

That adverse criticism was meted out to him in his own time with no stinted hand, is some excuse for the bitterness of his preface. Isaac Ware (Surveyor to King George) says : " It is our misfortune at this time to see

an unmeaning scrawl of C's, inverted and looped together, taking the place
of Greek and Roman elegance, even in our most expensive decorations.
It is called French, and let them have the praise of it. The Gothic
shaft and Chinese bell are not beyond nor below it in poorness of
imagination." No wonder that Isaac Ware, who, in 1750, was still
ornamenting his chimneypieces with classic urns and pediments in heaviest

FIG. 17.—"RIBBAND BACK" CHAIR.   Chippendale.

Queen Anne style, was horrified at the flamboyant copies of French
mirrors and girandoles to which Chippendale devoted himself at the
outset of his career.

It is chiefly as a master of chairs that Chippendale has come down to us,
and as they occupy the first twenty pages of the *Director*, we may argue
that he himself placed them above his other designs. The merest glance
will suffice to show how largely he depended for his earlier ornament on
the fashions prevailing on the Continent at the time, though gradually its

derivation became less obvious as the extravagances were toned down and blended. Some of the designs are almost identical with their French originals, as far as the ornament is concerned, but the foundations upon which it is imposed are English in shape and make. Enough of the previous Dutch character is retained to render the seats sufficiently roomy to accommodate the ladies' hoops, and the stiffened coat skirts of the men. Even the broad

FIG. 18.—CHIPPENDALE CHAIR.   FIG. 19.—CHIPPENDALE CHAIR.

back, bandy leg, and claw and ball foot are preserved, though beautified with rococo carving. The arms too are often richly decorated with lions' or goats' heads, dolphins, or dragons, though the well-known curved endive and scroll work is more common.

Chippendale borrowed largely from Louis Quatorze ornament for the "ribband back" chairs, which he numbered among his best work, saying, "If I may speak without vanity," they "are the best I have ever seen (or perhaps have ever been made)." In these he may have ignored all the principles laid down by the exponents of pure design, and represented wood tied into different shapes in the most unstructural manner, yet the various ways in which he expressed this graceful form very nearly attained perfection. The skill inherent in his family is displayed in the wonderful carving, which, notwithstanding the varied sources from which it was

FIG. 20.—GOTHIC TABLE AND CHAIR, from Lacock Abbey. Chippendale.

derived, is always fresh and graceful. Chippendale, thoroughly eclectic in taste, mixed French, Gothic, and Chinese in one harmonious whole. The effect is so perfect that his furniture requires no further enrichment by inlay or painting. This is a point which cannot be too strongly emphasised. Both had been used before his day, and his avoidance of them is characteristic of the man. He saw everything with a carver's eye, and so in love was he with his craft that, except for gilding, occasional brass ornamenting, and japanning, the chisel remained his only mistress.

He had many imitators not only in his own time, but in subsequent years, and much which is now known by his name in reality belonged to them. This is not only unjust to other workers, but is still more unfair to Chippendale himself. When we meet with chairs

FIG. 21.—GOTHIC HALL-CHAIR, in the possession of Sir W. Fitzherbert. . Chippendale.

undoubtedly his work, treasured in the same family for over a century, we can see at once how they won so high a place in public estimation. Not only are they thoroughly serviceable, but the workmanship and carving are complete in rich effect and beauty of detail. The ornament on the cabriole legs and frames is as delicate as that in the backs, while the proportions of both are equally well balanced. Very different are they from the squat forms and ungainly shapes of Manwaring, Ince, Mayhew, and other chair-makers.

The interlacing tracery of some of the open backs has a decided resemblance to church windows, from which the idea may originally have been taken. Still stronger expression of ecclesiastical styles can be found in his Gothic chairs, chiefly used to furnish halls, like those from Lacock Abbey; for Horace Walpole's "Gothic Vatican of Greece and Rome" at Strawberry Hill led many to copy this attempted revival. Even initials

FIG. 22.—CHINESE CHAIR. Chippendale.   FIG. 23.—CHINESE CHAIR. Chippendale.

were sometimes used to fill the backs, as in a set at Lyme, where the monogram of the Martyr King forms the tracery.

The chairs which Chippendale designed to suit the widespreading Chinese movement have not only irregular lattice-work and pierced frets, but also the square leg which drove out the really Chinese curvilinear for a time. It was, no doubt, the utility of construction which appealed to Chippendale's practical turn of mind, and led him to adopt this form of support. He describes his chairs "after the Chinese manner" as "very proper for a lady's dressing-room, especially if hung with India paper, and they will likewise suit Chinese tempels."

The name "French," which Chippendale gives to several of his chairs, refers to the upholstery rather than the design, for in these early days stuffed chairs were French chairs, no matter whether the woodwork was in the rococo style or not.

It is difficult now to say what material Chippendale most frequently adopted for the coverings of his stuffed chairs, stools, and sofas, as many of

FIG. 24.—FRENCH CHAIR.   Chippendale.

these were afterwards upholstered afresh to suit altered fashions.   The workers of this time excelled in the surprising exactness with which they copied pictures for screens and other furniture, and many of his best chairs, when found in their original condition, have seats of worsted close-stitch in flowers, geometric patterns, or figure designs.   Besides this needlework, he alludes to tapestry, Spanish leather, and damask, fastened down by mouldings, or rows of brass nails, and especially comments on the fine effect red morocco will produce.

"Darby and Joan seats," or settees made up of two or more chairs, were frequently constructed to match the different styles, though Chippendale has no such designs in his book. His stuffed-back sofas are more inviting and restful than these, as the decoration is mainly carved on the legs and lower part, considerations of comfort shutting it out from the upper. His "state sofa" is, however, an exception: "emblems of rest, assiduity, and watchfulness," in the form of cupids, clouds, and eagles, are placed

FIG. 25.—SETTEE made for the Bury Family of Kateshill, Bewdley, which, with the corresponding chairs, are covered with old needlework.   Chippendale.

above the cushioned back.   Whenever "grand" or "state" designs appear, an immense amount of allegorical ornament was used to pander to the decorative foibles of the day.

A large portion of the *Director* is taken up with drawings for bed-pillars and beds, and Chippendale remembered his five orders sufficiently to introduce their shafts and capitals.   The wreaths of flowers and twisted ribbons make some of the posts especially beautiful, but the designs for entire beds are very elaborate—pagoda tops, sunk Gothic panels, and rococo ornament being often all employed on one canopy.   These gorgeous beds can only be regarded as high-flown advertisements, for though there can be no doubt that the whole school of designers turned out beautiful

FIG. 26.—STUFFED SOFA. Chippendale.

FIG. 27.—SOFA. Chippendale.

and practical four-posters in large quantities, their published designs for complete beds seem only intended to realise the descriptions in the inflated

romances of the period, and Chippendale's
Gothic beds are more suited to the Castle
of Otranto than an eighteenth-century
house. The state beds, like much of
Chippendale's finer furniture, were evidently intended for gilding. The gold
was so well laid on, and so many coatings
often given to the wood, that even now,
in many cases, it retains its original lustre.
As a rule, ordinary Chippendale furniture
was constructed of mahogany, which was
particularly well suited to his style of
treatment, and the high polish attainable
with oil and rubbing further enhanced
its value. This wood, though discovered
by Sir Walter Raleigh, had only come into
general use about 1720, and very soon, to
Dr. Johnson's great disgust, quite dis-
placed the oak and walnut of the previous
century. Its first introduction to this
country was as a medicinal substitute for
" Jesuit's Bark," some planks having been
sent to a Dr. Gibbon by his brother, a
West India captain, for this purpose.
Having more than he required, he proposed using the remainder for building,
but the carpenters objected to the wood
on account of its hardness. The doctor
then wished a candle-box to be made out
of it, and insisted on this being done.
The article was so much admired that a
bureau was next attempted, which all
London came to see. Mr. G. T. Robinson,
in the *Art Journal*, suggests that this
candle-box revolutionised English furniture, for both construction and design
were altered by the introduction of

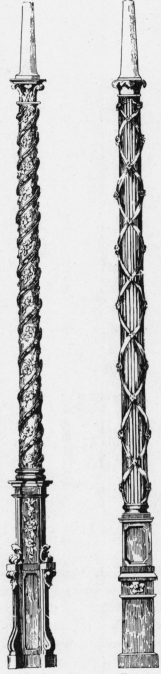

FIG. 28.   FIG. 29.
CHIPPENDALE BED-POSTS.

mahogany.   Owing to its toughness and durability furniture could be made much lighter and more delicate in appearance, and yet as able to withstand changes of temperature, and wear and tear, as the heavier

FIG. 30.—GILDED STAND FOR A
CHINA JAR.   Chippendale.

FIG. 31.—CHINA-CASE, illustrating the three styles combined.
Chippendale.

native woods formerly employed.   Chippendale exercised the greatest care in the selection of his material, and that is one of the reasons why his chairs and cabinets possess such beauty and durability.   In this selection he had advantages which can never occur again.   Mahogany was a comparatively recent discovery, and there were immense tracts of

FIG. 32.—SCREEN, illustrating the three styles combined. Chippendale.

FIG. 33.—FIRE-SCREEN, mainly in the Louis Quinze style. Chippendale.

FIG. 34.—FIRE-SCREEN of combined French styles. Chippendale.

untouched primeval forests yielding wood of a beauty and quality which it would now be quite impossible to match.

The foundation of Chippendale's cabinets, bookcases, and larger woodwork was generally classic, but when he had attended to the general

FIG. 35.—WARDROBE WITH WREATHED PEDIMENT.　Chippendale.

proportion, he considered himself at liberty to run into any eccentricity in the way of ornament.　A good deal of this freedom arose from the use of the Louis Quinze style, but Chippendale did not exclusively tie himself down to any one time or country, but combined such seeming incongruities as the scroll ornament, pagoda top, and sunk panels in the

cabinet and fire-screen here illustrated.   It must, however, be remembered
to his credit that he succeeded, as far as success was possible, where so many
have failed.   The result is far from displeasing, for he instinctively used

FIG. 36.—GOTHIC BOOKCASE.   Chippendale.

only such parts of the styles as had most points of resemblance.   In
screens and other furniture the *motif* is entirely French, though Louis
Quinze does not reign alone, for Chippendale's earlier love for the style of
" le grand Monarque" revives every here and there.

Mouldings, carved wood, and fretwork formed the decoration of the
cabinets and bookcases, while a pediment was generally placed upon the
top.   In the less elaborate pieces it was of the interrupted scroll order, but

frequently burst into florid wreaths and flowers in the more fantastic designs, like those on the wardrobe (Fig. 35) and the writing-table illustrated in the

FIG. 37.—CHINA-CABINET, enclosing Chinese Casket. Belonging to Sir E. Hope Verney, of Claydon House, Bucks.

frontispiece. The glass panels in the doors were broken up into all sorts of shapes by carved scroll mouldings, though the work on the commoner furniture was confined to geometrical forms. Sometimes Chippendale

departed entirely from his close imitation of French fashions to design
bookcases in the most pointed Gothic style to suit houses where that spirit
was cultivated either wholly or in part.   One design is nearly identical

FIG. 38.—CHINA-SHELVES.   Chippendale.

with those made for Horace Walpole's library, which were "taken from a
side doorcase to the choir in Dugdale's St. Paul's." Though few rooms
were so Gothic as this, where the chimney-piece was taken from a tomb
in Westminster Abbey, and the ceiling painted by Clermont from another
at Canterbury, still, walls were often decorated in Gothic design or stone-

coloured paper used, with a wooden dado tinted the same colour to heighten the ecclesiastical effect.

The Chinese style was appropriately adopted by Chippendale for his china cases and cabinets: quaint conceits with pagoda or dome tops, bells,

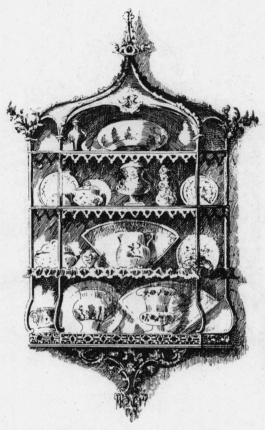

FIG. 39.—HANGING CHINA-SHELVES. Chippendale.

and fretwork, like that belonging to Sir E. Hope Verney (Fig. 37). In this the delicate mahogany framework encloses a red lacquer Chinese cabinet, but they were more frequently filled with the china or delft which the Dutch taste of William and Mary's court had imported. Even in Queen Anne's reign the merchants and well-to-do people had furniture invented to show off their china, and the rage became so great that Hogarth held it up to popular ridicule. The mania served one good purpose. It roused Chippendale to even greater efforts in designing shelves, tables, and stands in every conceivable shape and taste for the display of these treasures. The art may not always have been of the best, but the furniture was singularly well suited to its purpose. Great attention was paid even to the smaller pieces. Each little fret was separately designed, and though the detail often varied, the unity of the whole was well

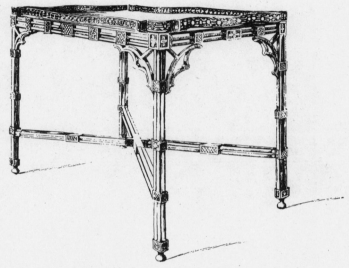

FIG. 40.—CHINA-TABLE, belonging to C. H. Talbot, Esq. Chippendale.

preserved. When these are contrasted with modern imitations, the beauty of the work and the fine wood selected make it possible for even a tyro to distinguish between them.

Many of Chippendale's designs would have been beneath notice had it not been for his eye for general contour. No matter how wildly mixed the styles might be, the graceful outline carried them through. Manwaring and Mayhew, on the other hand, were Chippendales without a sense of form. They loaded the outline with superfluous ornament, forgetting the symmetry which was the essence of the whole. So careful was Chippendale in this particular that he advised workmen to make a model of the design before beginning.

Sideboards seem to have been English institutions from an early date, for they are mentioned as early as 1553. These were not what we understand by the term, but literally *sideboards*, without drawers or cupboards. Chippendale's designs are entirely for this form of table, generally from five to six feet long, and two feet eight inches high, with as many legs as the size demanded. The ornament varied. In some cases frets were glued

Fig. 41.—Sideboard Table and Tea-chest. Chippendale.

on to the solid wood, while in others, the square legs and the fronts were cut completely through to give them a lighter appearance. The wooden or marble tops served to accommodate the accessories of the dinner-table, for it belonged to the architects of the day to provide cupboards where the glass and china could be stowed away behind the numerous doors it was then the custom to introduce into every room, for fashion decreed uniformity, and the entrances had to be symmetrically balanced. The

FIG. 42.—CHIMNEY-PIECE, WITH STOVE GRATE, MIRROR, FIRE-SCREEN, AND CHINA-TABLE.   Chippendale.

bare look of these tables, as well as their insufficiency of accommodation, caused various conveniences to be gradually added.

The "tea-chest" placed upon the sideboard in the sketch will give an idea of what Chippendale devised to hold the precious commodity, then very fashionable in spite of its expense. These caddies were rather large in size, and intended to have "ornaments of silver or brass." Hepplewhite, thirty years later, provided daintier but hardly more beautiful cases of coloured woods to contain the silver or Battersea enamel "teapoys" for green or black tea.

FIG. 43.—TEA-KETTLE STAND. Chippendale.

The bureau, common long before this date, was often used in bedrooms to contain clothes, as well as papers and writing materials. It was frequently substituted for a dressing - table, so it is natural to find Chippendale designing dressing - tables mainly of the "buroe" type. His "lady's-toilet table" has, however, a mirror attached, with cupboards on each side, very much like the modern Duchesse style. An elaborate arrangement of festooned damask with gilded cupid cornices is much in the style we see in Hogarth's pictures, and, with embroidered draperies, was greatly used at the time. In striking contrast are the folding shaving-tables of plain mahogany for gentlemen's dressing-rooms. These are of richly marked wood, plain and solid, while every part is well finished. In the original of our sketch, the glass rises on a spring catch but falls into the back of the table when not required, the flaps fold across, and there has originally been a sunk basin before the glass between the two compartments for shaving utensils. Chippendale also gives designs for "tripod basin-

FIG. 44.—SHAVING-TABLE. Chippendale.

stands," some plain like the one illustrated, others embellished with rococo carving. There is indeed such diversity among the kinds of Chippendale furniture that it can hardly have been the work of one hand. More likely the family as well as assistants were employed in these wholly dissimilar styles; some having charge of the graceful gilded chimney-pieces, others of the fret ornament, while Chippendale himself is generally credited with the delicate carving.

Many of the designs in the *Director* were never worked out, or were shorn of their more expensive decoration in the working. The plates give the main elements of the style, though they do not come so near what was actually made as those of Hepplewhite and Sheraton. The more ornate furniture would be quite out of the reach of any but the

FIG. 45.—TRIPOD- BASIN-STAND.
Chippendale.

FIG. 46.—CHIPPENDALE WASH-STAND
MODERNISED.

wealthiest, and is now only to be found in museums or the houses of the nobility. As the Chippendale furniture which has come down to us consists chiefly of chairs, fretted tables, screens, and bookcases, of the plainer kind, it is probable that these were made in larger numbers, while the grander specimens were only executed to special order. He often adds to his description of a plate that he would "have much pleasure in the execution of it," while the same article is sometimes drawn in various degrees of embellishment, from the severest outline to the most lavish French rococo.

Chippendale's wall decoration possesses more originality than some of his work. Though he adopted much of the broken scroll and shell-shaped woodwork used in France, he added a wealth of extraordinary detail. Long-beaked birds, rockwork, and dripping water, Chinese figures and pagodas, or whole scenes from *Æsop's Fables*, decorate the mirrors and overmantels. These, carved in pine, were thickly gilt, with the more prominent parts burnished. To save expense, the mirrors were often fitted up in three plates, and the joints covered with small gilt mouldings or pilasters. The unequal way in which the glass was thus broken up produced a quaint effect, which, careless and fantastic

FIG. 47.—PIER-GLASS FRAME.   Chippendale.

though it may appear, was always carefully planned to help the general outline. In this lies the chief difference between Chippendale's oft-copied mirrors and those of his school. Johnson's overloaded and ill-placed

FIG. 48.—GIRANDOLE. Chippendale.

ornament is what catches and holds the eye; while in Chippendale, though we may smile at the affected fancies in passing, the glance is carried at once to the fine form of the whole. In the same way, though his tiny girandoles are often made up of architectural ruins, the essential lightness and grace are never in one instance lost.

The thin plates of Vauxhall glass in these mirror-frames had a delicate pinky hue, and the soft narrow bevel, ground by hand, was necessarily very flat, constituting its chief charm. This, notwithstanding the many convolutions of the carving, followed every twist and turn of the frame.

Some of the designs, both in the *Director* and other books, appear to indicate that the glass panels of some of the mirrors and cabinets were embellished by engraving and "back-painting"; the painting and silvering being on the same side. Mezzotints were sometimes transferred to the glass, and touched up with colour; but landscapes, frequently Chinese, were attempted by the more skilled artists, much after the manner of Zenner, who invented and practised the art of combined painting and etching in gold and silver leaf about the middle of the century.

It is generally supposed that Chippendale confined his attention entirely to wood, but cisterns, hall "lanthorns," and chandeliers were not forgotten, and brass ornamented stove grates are shown in the fireplace designs, as well as separately. These, like the pages of brass handles and escutcheons, were all in the florid French style he so loved to render. Undoubtedly Chippendale, as well as the other carvers of the day, was strongly influenced by the Continental schools. The mere fact of their descriptions being often repeated in French proves that they were acquainted with that language; and, whether they travelled or not, they must have read and assimilated the works of the French designers. From the lines of his clock-cases, it is almost certain that Chippendale must have seen those published by Morot at Amsterdam in 1702, and his commodes and commode-tables might stand for representative work of the contemporary French schools. The wave of Renaissance which had swept over the Continent could hardly fail to affect our countrymen. But every country altered the Renaissance to suit the characteristics of its people; and Chippendale, though he felt its influence, and in many cases derived his inspiration from it, adapted it till it became a style of his own. He never sought to disguise that he often took his designs from the French with very little alteration, as the French had received theirs from Italy. Chippendale, with an honesty as rare in his day as in our own, distinctly calls many of his designs French, and entitles his merely commonplace work *Sconces, Chimney and Looking-glass Frames, in the old French style.* He is widely accused of lack of originality, but in the truest sense of the word, that of leaving the impress of his mind on

everything he did, he is without doubt original.   He took, for instance,
the Queen Anne chair, kept what was beautiful in its lines and curves, and,
adding thereto designs inspired by another school, produced a homogeneous
and beautiful whole, which was as much his own creation as it is in the
nature of any art creation to be.   That he was influenced by many men and
schools is simply to say that he was catholic in his tastes, and, with a

FIG. 49.—COMMODE CLOTHES-PRESS.   Chippendale.

receptivity which is by no means too common, not only kept his mind
open to what was good in the work of other people, but allowed what
appealed to him to enter into his own.   Compare the Queen Anne chair
with a typical example of Chippendale.   The same structure will be found
in both, for he preserved the high back and cabriole leg of the Dutch
school.   Before his time the plain back had been pierced first with a
heart-shaped opening, gradually developing into more intricate ornament.
Even suggestions of scroll carving were in some cases added here and on
the top, so that Chippendale chairs, as we know them, may quite well have

been simply evolutions from the English chair in use when he began his labours.

It is impossible to overlook the enormous improvement Chippendale effected on English furniture as he found it.   In the few engravings of

FIG. 50.—CABINET.   Chippendale.

social life in the reign of Queen Anne, the bare look of the appointments is astonishing.   A table in the centre, a few high-backed and clumsy chairs, a square box-like settee, a picture or two on the walls, sometimes, not always, a looking-glass, and occasionally an alcove with shelves for bric-a-brac or china.   Except in the houses of the nobility, there was little really good furniture, beyond imported Chinese or Dutch lacquer.   What

it often was in Pope's time we may gather from a letter addressed to the
Duke of Buckingham, describing the contents of the great parlour of an old
house in which he was staying in the first half of the century as "a broken-
bellied virginal, a couple of crippled velvet chairs, with two or three
mildewed pictures of mouldy ancestors" looking down from their frames.
Even in Hogarth's painting of "Marriage à la Mode," the tasteless furniture
and ornaments in the gorgeous saloon (all designed by Kent) will give
some idea of the "barrenness of the land" into which Chippendale was
born.

FIG. 51.—QUEEN ANNE CHAIR.

FIG. 52.—QUEEN ANNE CHAIR, with pierced
opening and slight carving.

It is in chairs that Chippendale most excels.   His designs are, one and
all, marvels of beauty both as regards line and spacing.   He spent as much
thought and consideration on the space left at each side of what is tech-
nically known as the "splat," or central part of the back of a chair, as he
did on the splat itself.   The space so left is always carefully considered,
and is as beautiful a piece of design as if the chair had been made with
this one object.   This may seem a very small matter, but it is really of
the first importance, and is generally forgotten by modern adapters of
Chippendale's style.

Most critics have taken exception to his ribbon-backed chairs on the ground that wood is not the proper material in which to represent ribbon. This is, however, merely a return to the first principle of design, as shown in the early Celtic stone-work, in which the pattern is evidently copied from two or more looped or knotted interlacing strings. In Chippendale we find the material that suggested the design more realistically reproduced, but as that is a fault from which we, a century or more later, have not yet succeeded in emancipating ourselves, the less we say about it the better. It does not become people who walk on carpets which, if not covered with the realistic roses of the past, are still strewn with unmistakable flowers, to object to the ribbon on the back of a chair constructed a hundred and twenty years ago.

In looking at his work as a whole, we must always remember that, though an artist, he was trammelled, like other artists, by the taste of his time. As he says in the *Director*, his designs are intended to suit the " fancy and circumstances of persons in all degrees of life." The mere business side could not by any possibility be left out, and if there was a demand, fostered by Sir William Chambers, for objects in the Chinese style, the blame belongs to Chambers and others more than to Chippendale, if that demand was supplied. The fashion was already there, and continued in vogue till long after. Rooms were decorated in it and pagodas built, so furniture was naturally a necessity. If his detractors are right in saying that Chippendale ought not to have supplied Chinese furniture for a Chinese room, it would be instructive to hear what he should really have created for the purpose. As a trader, moreover, he was compelled to trade in such articles as were likely to sell, and all that lay in his power was to make them as artistic as their nature would allow.

Objections have been made to the heaviness of Chippendale's furniture, and indeed the designs of Hepplewhite and Sheraton were more or less protests against it. It is very easy to say that Chippendale's designs remind one of the time when furniture might, at any moment, be used as a weapon of offence or defence, but there is a solidity and honesty about it, which, when combined with graceful curves and well-studied proportion, quite make up for any lack of lightness.

It was not only an *appearance* of strength that satisfied Chippendale. He was careful that each piece of furniture, of whatever kind, should be constructive from a mechanical point of view. In a chair, for example, it is evident that the greatest strain is likely to be at the point where the back joins the framework of the seat, because it is there that the leverage is greatest. Even in his most florid designs, Chippendale is always careful that the splat should help to strengthen this weakest part. In Hepplewhite and Sheraton we find that the splat seldom runs into the body of the chair, and never in their more distinctive designs. In the "shield back" chair, which is Hepplewhite's favourite shape, the shield and its interior ornament making the splat never touch the seat of the chair at all. Sheraton used this form in the same way, and in the square shapes both he and Hepplewhite ran the splat, not into the framework of the seat, but into a small horizontal rail some inches above it. The only possible reason for this is a bad one. It is evident that by thus transgressing mechanical rules, a feeling of lightness approaching to fragility is obtained, but it is obtained at an actual cost of strength. Some of Hepplewhite's oval designs sin even more in this particular. One of his "parlour chairs," for instance, is of the lightest possible make wherever there is necessity for strength, and heavy wherever there is no necessity for anything but lightness. The oval back and all four legs are so light that one's first idea on seeing the design is that it would be hardly safe for a man of twelve or thirteen stone to risk sitting upon it. To this he superadds a particularly heavy central feather in the oval, which, while still further reducing the apparent weight of the framework, gives the chair a top-heavy look. There are only two explanations to these facts. Either Sheraton and Hepplewhite knew nothing, and cared less, about the principles of construction, or they purposely broke what rules they knew to give a fictitious appearance of lightness to their work.

But Chippendale's strength is required from the use to which the object is to be put, and where lightness occurs there is no probability of any great strain. By a careful and skilful choice of well-seasoned wood, and by making strength and durability his motto, he produced articles which are, many of them, still whole and sound, and which, with anything like ordinary care, will go down to succeeding centuries as marvels of constructive thought and workmanlike ability.

So careful was he to make his furniture durable, that when the rage for fretwork came in, he would not carve the frets out of one piece of wood on account of the liability to breakage. He glued several thin pieces of wood together, with the grain running in different directions, thus forming a thin

slip of immense strength from the fact that one " way " of the grain pro-
tected each of the others.

But strength and beauty were not the only things considered by
Chippendale. The use for which the object was intended was always kept
in mind. Even in his most flamboyant chairs, there is a carefully planned
structure on which the ornament is super-imposed. From the shape and
height of the back, to the proportions of the seat and the position of the
arms, nothing was too small for the great carver to plan. One of the chief
differences between his chairs and those of Sheraton and Hepplewhite is
that Chippendale's are intended first for use, and secondly for show ;
whereas the chairs of his successors are often very beautiful, but by no
means so comfortable.

One curious point is that the greater part of Chippendale's reputation
was in all likelihood posthumous ; for Lyon, in his researches for his work
on *Colonial Furniture*, found that Chippendale's name never occurs in
inventories of the time. Even Walpole, who left so many interesting
memoranda concerning other designers and decorators, never alludes to him.
Though the style was not entirely created by Chippendale, it afterwards
came to be called by his name, to the utter exclusion of others who had
contributed largely to the movement. Since the renaissance of taste for
later eighteenth-century furniture, other names have been again recalled,
though it must be admitted that no one could place them on the same
plane as the Master Craftsman of the century.

That Chippendale was influenced by French taste is indisputable ; but
there is every difference between being influenced and stealing a style
wholesale. No great artist has ever lived who was not influenced by the
work that went before him ; in fact, it may be taken as a general rule that
the greater the artist the greater is his power of absorption. Nor is style
a thing formed by one man. It is generally the growth of centuries, and
reaches its culminating point in some exceptional genius, who, from being
its chief exponent, generally gives his name to the school, though in many
cases he was not the originator even of the particular departure for which
he is known. But however " original " a style may be, it is always easy to
trace its source. Take, for example, the two great painters who broke most
away from the lines of their predecessors. Raphael and Rembrandt were
as unmistakably Italian and Dutch in their styles as if they had never
made a departure from the convention of their periods. This was very

greatly due to the difficulty of travel. Where we find a great artist like Vandyke travelling from country to country, we also find the influence of the art of these countries in his work. " And yet I have never been to Rome," said Rembrandt to Vandyke. " So I perceive," was the reply ; for Vandyke knew, from his own experience, how impossible it is for the true artist to see and really appreciate the best work of other schools without showing it in his own.

This is forgotten by the hosts of detracting critics who are always ready to prove theft by any means that comes first to hand. An instance of this is the curious manner in which one writer proves Chippendale's indebtedness to the French, by telling us that the eagle's claw holding a ball belongs to the reign of Louis Quatorze. Yet this, and the quotation given from Ware, are examples of the unfair criticism which, both in his own time and in ours, has been heaped on Chippendale's work. To any one who has given even a superficial attention to the subject, such statements are simply ridiculous. In his utter incapacity to understand anything but straight lines, Ware calls Chippendale's multitudinous and graceful curves " an unmeaning scrawl of C's inverted and hooked together" ; while, let us hope in ignorance, one of his modern detractors accuses him, among other sins, of stealing from a French book the ancient Chinese emblem of dragon-claw and pearl, dating at least as far back as A.D. 254, and well known both in Holland and England long before Chippendale's time.

The reason of this is not far to seek. Let us compare the furniture which came before Chippendale with that which came after, and there can be no doubt in any one's mind that meantime an immense advance had been made. Except, indeed, where the post-Chippendale designers relied entirely on their own taste, there is no comparison between the two periods. Chippendale, who saw neither the beginning nor the end of the renaissance, is, in more senses than one, the central figure of the whole movement, and rightly does this great period of English design bear his name. He is the king of eighteenth-century furniture designers, and if abuse has been heaped upon his head, it is because of

> That fierce light which beats upon a throne,
> And blackens every blot.

IV

CHIPPENDALE'S CONTEMPORARIES

THE art wave of the Chippendale era resembled all other art waves in not being solely due to the work or influence of any one man. The same causes that called Chippendale into existence created also many others. What he did was to join together an infinity of ripples, some with real purpose, others apparently a mere troubling of the waters, into one gigantic movement.

Of the men who were working at the time, the chief names are Manwaring, Ince and Mayhew, Copeland, Lock, Johnson, and Crunden. There may have been, and very possibly were, others quite as distinguished as workmen, whose names are lost, because they did not, like those mentioned, publish illustrated books of their designs. Even in the case of the better-known men, we cannot, without the identification of any particular piece of furniture with their designs, be certain, except in the more typical pieces, to which of them we owe it, as the same characteristics of detail and ornament run through all. Some are almost exactly similar to Chippendale's, and are often classed as his work. This is the natural outcome of the lines Chippendale and the best of his contemporaries laid down for themselves. Their published books were, of course, intended to be in the first place an advertisement for their own work, but they were also meant for use by the trade at large, and there is no doubt that the permission to copy any or all of the designs was largely taken advantage of by the numbers of cabinet-makers, "upholders," joiners, and carvers whose forgotten names appear amongst the subscribers to his work. Except, therefore, in the rare instances where absolutely authentic articles exist, it is not from their furniture, but from their books, that we can judge their relative positions. With these before us, it is perfectly easy, from an artistic point of view, to place Chippendale and his contemporaries. Like Saul, he towers a head and shoulders above the people. Chronologically, however, it is by no means so easy to arrange their names. We have no convenient Pepys to gossip in their shops and provide us with little tit-bits of information; and Boswell, who might have helped us, was too much engaged in chronicling the sayings and doings of the great lexicographer. We know nothing of the men, not even when they were born and when they died. The only facts at our command regarding their periods are stray designs, or the dates of their published books. Even this is sometimes denied to us, as in the case both of the Society of Upholsterers, and Ince and Mayhew, whose volumes are undated. With regard to the former, the probability is that the publication of their work was anterior to that of Chippendale, but from this it would be manifestly unfair to argue an influence on Chippendale's style. The probability, indeed, is all on the other side. The designs of Manwaring and his collaborators have all the internal evidence of bad copies, and we must remember that the house of Chippendale had been in existence for many years before the publication of his book. Though, as he tells us, many of the designs given by him had yet to be worked out, the greater part must have been in existence, not merely as drawings, but as absolute pieces of furniture which could be, and probably were, seen by every member of the trade in London.

The book published by the Society of Upholsterers and Cabinet-makers is entitled *One Hundred New and Genteel Designs, being all the most approved Patterns of Household Furniture in the present taste.* The unformed state of the drawings would seem to suggest that it appeared before its authors had had the opportunity of studying the *Director.* Probably both were issued very nearly together, for a second edition of the Society's work came out before the *Chairmaker's Guide,* by R. Manwaring and others, in 1766, which, with a few more designs added, is simply a partial reprint. Prior to this (1765) the *Cabinet and Chairmaker's Real Friend and Companion* had appeared, for which Manwaring alone held himself responsible. The rapidly repeated editions, both of these and Chippendale's *Director,* bear evidence to the increasing interest then being taken in the improvement of furniture design; indeed, in the *Chairmaker's Friend* there is a long list of illustrated manuals advertised by the publisher Webley.

Manwaring appears to have been the leading spirit, but it is likely that Chippendale had a good deal to do with the Society to begin with, for the primal idea throughout is taken from his work, though the form is only weakly imitated. This strong resemblance gives colour to the supposition that Chippendale belonged to the Society at first, but from some unknown cause broke away from it to publish for himself. There are traces of the earlier condition of the style in the plain chair-backs, simply cut through, without ornament or carving, such as Chippendale himself gives in one of

FIG. 53.—WRITING TABLE.   Society of Upholsterers.

his plates; for the style did not rise, Minerva-like, from a single brain, but passed through stages of progressive evolution. In the same way the cabinet-makers had only arrived at the skeleton of the writing-table, which Chippendale's touch woke to life and beauty. The simplicity of the earlier design also appears in a bookcase whose plain and severe outline is repeated several times in varying ways, shaming the commonplace and badly drawn copies of French curves and Chippendale ornament in the surrounding pages. Had the members of the Society contented themselves with this plainer work, and not aimed at imitating the genius they could not approach, they would have had better claim to our praise. The dissimilarity of styles in the designs proves how many hands and minds contributed, but the names of the designers are unfortunately omitted. Manwaring must have contributed the chairs, for they are almost as bad as those in his own book.   Every sort and kind are devised to supply the want which the improved conditions of domestic life were demanding. Parlour, dining-room, hall, Gothic and Chinese, are provided, but not even one of real merit can be found.   The outline is in all cases ungainly, and

FIG. 54.—OPEN PEDIMENT BUREAU AND BOOKCASE.
Society of Upholsterers.

FIG. 55.—STAND FOR CHINA JAR.
Society of Upholsterers.

the due proportions of the different parts entirely forgotten.   Chippendale may have impregnated the Society with his views, but he could have had nothing to do with their design ; for, though many, like the ribbon back illustrated (Fig. 57), are founded on his ideas, everything is omitted which he would have been careful to remember.   The chairs, taken altogether, are plainer than Chippendale's, and suggest the transition period when the English chair was being built up, and perforated wood for the backs was beginning to take the place of cane.   English chairs meant wooden chairs, for this school of design let France have the whole credit of the different varieties of upholstered seat.   "French" chairs and "French" stools, with

and without backs, corner seats and burjairs, were all more or less successful attempts at arriving at an easy and comfortable stuffed arm-chair.

Walpole had so stimulated the Gothic style of house decoration that
no book of the day was complete without a few such cabinets, doors, and
"embattled bookcases." The presence of these in the Society's work is
sufficient to account for a copy of that and Manwaring's other works
being included in the Strawberry Hill Library, but the drawing of

FIG. 56.—GOTHIC PARLOUR CHAIR.
Society of Upholsterers.

FIG. 57.—RIBBON-BACK CHAIR.
Society of Upholsterers.

most of the illustrations is so crude that only the dearth of previous
literature of the kind can explain the rapid sale.

The fourth and last part of the book is devoted to metal work, all
much better drawn and designed than the rest of the contents. The
vine-patterned railings and balconies, inn signs, and lamp obelisks are
such as still linger outside old houses in the neighbourhood of London;
while the wrought-iron door-tops are both interesting and pretty.

Turning to Manwaring's avowed work, we find the same "genteel"
designs repeated, though we might prefer a little more originality and
a little less gentility. The few ideas for chairs evolved since the

Society's work was printed are decidedly more ornamental, but considerably worse in every other particular. The best are but bad, and the worst beneath contempt. The "Rural" are simply branches of trees

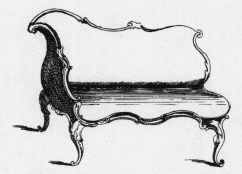

FIG. 58.--FRENCH CORNER CHAIR.   Society of Upholsterers.

twisted into fantastic shapes, and "may be made with limbs of yew and apple trees as nature produces them." Manwaring claims that they are " the first *designs* of rural chairs for summer-houses and temples, gardens and parks, which have ever been published," conveniently

FIG. 59.—FRENCH STOOL.   Society of Upholsterers.

forgetting those published by Chippendale in 1762. The question of priority seems to have been the cause of a decided animus in Manwaring's mind, with which jealousy of his contemporary's superiority may have had something to do.

The Cabinet and Chairmaker's Real Friend and Companion, or

the whole system of Chairmaking made plain and easy, is utterly
without value. Manwaring says that, "though the art of chairmaking,
as well as cabinet-making, has been brought to great perfection, notwith-

FIG. 60.—LADY'S DESK, in the Gothic style.
Society of Upholsterers.

FIG. 61.—IRONWORK FOR INN SIGN.
Society of Upholsterers.

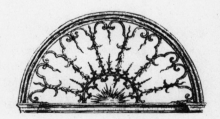

FIG. 62.—DOOR-TOP.
Society of Upholsterers.

standing which it will be ever capable of improvement, and though there
have appeared of late years several treatises and designs for household
furniture, some of which must be allowed by all artists to be of the
greatest utility in assisting their ideas for composing various designs,
yet upon the whole the practical workman has not been much instructed

in the execution of these designs, which appear to him so rich and
beautiful. The intent, therefore, of the following pages is to convey
to him full and plain instructions how to begin and finish with strength
and beauty all the designs that are advanced in this work." Unfortunately
he omits to inform the workman how he is to add the beauty in which
the designs are so singularly deficient, but merely adds that "they are
calculated for all people in different stations of life," and that "they
are actually originals and not pirated or copied from the designs or

FIG. 63.—RURAL CHAIR.   From "Cabinet-maker's Real Friend and Companion," by R. Manwaring.

inventions of others, which of late hath been too much practised,"
evidently referring to the plagiarism of which Chippendale was widely
accused.

The five orders of architecture must be dragged in somehow to a
book with such "genteel" pretensions, so, "with the advice of many
friends," he adds a geometrical view of their proportions, and informs
us "that, as a late very ingenious author says, (preface to Chippendale's
Designs for Household Furniture,) without an acquaintance with this
science, and some knowledge of the views of perspective, the cabinet-
maker cannot make the designs of his work intelligible, nor show in

a little compass the whole conduct and effect of the piece.   This, therefore, ought to be carefully studied by every one who would excel in this branch, since they are the very soul and basis of his art."

Strange to say, with all the advantage of this knowledge, Manwaring's designs have less claim to be considered than any of his contemporaries. The drawing in all cases is bad, and some of the designs are so very like Chippendale's, that, notwithstanding his disclaimers, it seems impossible

FIG. 64.—BEST CHAIR in Manwaring's   FIG. 65.—WORST CHAIR in Manwaring's
       " Chairmaker's Guide."   " Chairmaker's Guide."

for two minds to have created them independently.   We must therefore conclude that he founded his furniture on Chippendale's lines, and imitated all that was weakest in his master's style, without producing anything fresh and original, or even keeping the best of what he copied. He evidently did not expect his absurd ornament to be carried out, and, again imitating Chippendale, inserted it practically as an advertisement.   Regardless of common sense, he painted landscapes on his rustic seats, or, like Mayhew, wreathed some of the square legs of his Chinese chairs with floral carving.   Describing these, he says that "though they appear so elegant and superb, they are upon a very simple basis and may be easily executed. Should the ornamental parts be left out, the author has the boldness to assert that there will still remain *Grandeur* and *Magnificence*, and the design will still appear to be open and genteel." In fact, that last adjective describes his work better than any other. It was not fine, it was not original, it was not practical, it was only " genteel."

The books issued by Manwaring and the Society of Upholsterers were small in size, but Chippendale had set the fashion of large and

FIG. 66.—CHINESE CHAIR.   From Manwaring's " Chairmaker's Real Friend and Companion."

imposing volumes, with stilted prefaces and costly copperplates. Other folio volumes were issued in imitation of it during the next few years, more eccentric than Chippendale's, with none of its redeeming features. Size was frequently the only recommendation, and this is the case with the *Universal System of Household Furniture* emanating from Ince and Mayhew, cabinet-makers and " upholders," in Broad Street, Golden Square, " where every article in the several branches treated of is executed on the most reasonable terms, with the utmost neatness and punctuality." After this clever advertising on the title page, and a flowery dedication to the Duke of Marlborough, they tell us in the preface that "in furnishing all should be in propriety, elegance should always be joined with a peculiar neatness through the whole House, or otherwise immense Expense may be thrown away to no purpose, either in use or appearance; with the same regard any gentleman may furnish as neat at a small expense, as he can elegant and superb at a great one."

FIG. 67.—PARLOUR CHAIR.   Designed by W. Ince.

A "systematical order of raffle leaf from the line of beauty" is brought in to teach beginners drawing or carving by means of floral ornament, bearing witness that Hogarth's teaching of thirty years before had not been quite forgotten. The plates, of which a description is given both in French and English, were engraved by Darly, Chippendale's assistant, which may partially account for the great improvement on the engravings given by the Society of Upholsterers. But the articles are very nearly the same, and the fretwork ornament applied to the plain mahogany, the open-work backs to encoigneurs and china-shelves, the pagodas and mandarins, are identical in every respect. But Ince and Mayhew's book is a greater caricature of the Chippendale style, and far surpasses even his most flamboyant designs in the absurdity of the ornament introduced. A couch cannot be left alone, but, imitating the French, has to be endowed with a ridiculous and unnecessary canopy, and entitled "un grand Sofa."

The dome bed is a wild impossibility, with suns, clouds, rays, and cupids at the head and on the tester, while the hangings are of blue damask richly fringed with gold. As it might be doubted if such an extravagant design could be carried out, Ince is careful to tell us that "it has been

Fig. 68.—Burjair. By J. Mayhew.

executed, and may be esteemed amongst the best in England." That these gilded state beds were made for palaces and houses of the nobility is proved by several being still in existence, but they were not of everyday occurrence, like the mahogany four-posters, with their graceful pillars and beautiful carving. Even in Queen Anne's time, when little attention was paid to furnishing, the bed had been the most glorified piece of furniture in the house, and one was advertised in a lottery which "had two thousand ounces of gold and silver wrought in it." Though this was an extraordinary bed, still records tell us of velvet hangings and dome-crowned tops, like those in Hogarth's pictures of high life at the time. Many of Ince's designs are surmounted by plumes of feathers, either gilded or real, like the bed at Strawberry Hill "of purple cloth lined with white satin and a plume of white and purple feathers on the tester." In fact, much of the furniture in this book is in the style which Walpole affected, for he "did not make the house so Gothic as to exclude modern refinements in luxury," and the japanned

FIG. 69.—LADY'S SECRETAIRE.   Designed by W. Ince.

and gilded dressing-glasses, with damask draperies caught up by gilded ornaments, resemble his "blue bed-chamber with the toilette worked by Mrs. Clive." But Ince and Mayhew's furniture is not altogether intended to cater for the more extravagant tastes of the nobility, as the bed-stands, and chests of drawers, like the dressing-table illustrated, are reasonable and pretty. The card-tables, which the gambling habits of the day made too common, have places for counters and stands for candles, much the same as in the Upholsterers' book. In the "china-table, with shelf for books or china," Mayhew exhibits his ridiculous disposition to out-Chippendale Chippendale, without the least attempt to effect a pleasing whole. It is ultra-Chinese, because in similar furniture Chippendale affected the Chinese manner. It is more than probable that many absurdities, now attributed to Chippendale, owe their origin to Ince and Mayhew. In the side section

FIG. 70.—LADY'S DRESSING-TABLE. W. Ince.

of a Louis Quinze dressing-room for Lady Fludyer, as well as in the dressing and parlour chairs throughout the book, there is all the excessive ornament, without any of the symmetry and cohesion, of Chippendale's work. The important size, and presumably early date, may lend this volume a fictitious value, but it is mainly as a commentary on the work of the Master Cabinet-maker that it is of interest.

A story is told of a modern animal painter, who, at one time, copied Landseer so exactly that it was impossible to tell his best work from Landseer's worst. "Very like a Landseer," said a friend, on being asked for a criticism. "Ah yes," said the little man, swelling himself out, "Landseer and I just give and take." "How interesting," was the reply. "And—may I ask which of you does the giving, and which the taking?" There can be no difficulty in apportioning the giving and taking as regards these collaborators and Chippendale. They not only appropriated, but they committed the unforgivable sin of spoiling what they took. They copied their model too closely to fall into the constructive errors of Sheraton and Hepplewhite; but, on the other hand, they did not possess, like them, a feeling for grace and beauty of line.

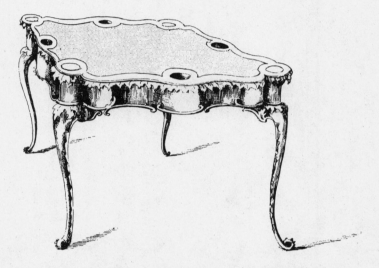

FIG. 71.—CARD-TABLE, with holes for counters and stands for candles.   Designed by W. Ince.

In Illustration 73, Fig. A is a sketch from Ince and Mayhew, which, though copied in each part from Chippendale, is so badly combined that it has nearly every fault that a design can well have. In the first place, the whole design is weakened by the accentuated use of convex curves. Chippendale was generally careful to avoid the convex, but Fig. B is a specimen from his *Director*, where he has made skilful use of it. The weakness of the sweeping convex curve is strengthened by its being divided into two on the lower side, which, besides adding strength to the design, gives it variety by adding another dimension. Even as it stands in the *Director* it is by no means the best of Chippendale's work, but it at least shows careful thought, and knowledge of the principles of design. Now

FIG. 72.—CHINA-TABLE, with shelf for books or china.   By J. Mayhew.

glance at the piracy of Ince and Mayhew. Because Chippendale put two curves on the inner side of his drawing, they differentiate theirs by putting three, and plainly show that they have not the faintest conception of *why* these curves were so placed, by dividing Chippendale's *one* upper curve into *three* weak ones, thereby making these repeat exactly the forms

A.—CHAIR-BACK. Ince and Mayhew.

B.—CHAIR-BACK. Chippendale.

C.—CHAIR-BACK. Chippendale.

FIG. 73.

on the lower side. As if this were not enough, they make the dimensions of the two curves that take us to what we may call the top corner of the chair as nearly as possible of the same length as the central ornament on the top rail—a mistake which Chippendale could never have made. In the model by Chippendale, we find that the curves on the inner side are balanced on the splat by a broken ornament, forming practically a straight line, thus avoiding any appearance of repeating the curves, and at the same time making a pleasant piece of spacing. But Ince and Mayhew go out of their way to do exactly the opposite, by super-imposing on their splat a most unnecessary piece of rococo ornament. The word "super-imposed" is used advisedly. They seemed to be utterly ignorant of the fact that ornament may have the value of a line. One glance at the drawing will show that, granting they could design at all, the structural line of their design was considerably inside the line made by this ornament, and that the ornament was an afterthought, which hid their first intention. This is never so in Chippendale's work, where the ornament is a part, and an integral part, of the design. Chippendale's use of ornament is very well exemplified by Fig. C. He never leaves it to tell alone, but strengthens it on the opposite side by a firm sweeping line, thus obtaining, even in his most intricate drawings, a look of simplicity and stability. Ince and Mayhew, on

FIG. 74.—VOIDER.   W. Ince.

the other hand, seem never to have had a reason for anything they did. In their utter incompetency, they used curves simply because Chippendale employed them, and larded them with rococo ornament for the same reason. But peace to their ashes! If they did nothing else, at least they triumphantly proved how great an artist Chippendale really was, by showing how small an alteration was needed to turn his designs into the commonplace and ridiculous.

Though Sir William Chambers was responsible for the somewhat too full recognition of the Chinese style, he was by no means the first to introduce it into Europe, or even into England. Both Dutch and English merchants had, for a century or more, been importing lacquer cabinets and oriental porcelain, particularly the latter, for the state of our own ceramic art was at a very low ebb. This had prepared the way for other articles of furniture, in which a considerable trade had been established. The introduction of tea, about the time of the Restoration, and the prominence given to the "China Drink" by the influence of Catherine of Braganza, the Queen of Charles II., had also much to do with the popularity of this style, so that the public mind was prepared to receive the dictum of the great architect.

Though Chambers is very generally credited (and probably with reason) with the sudden growth of the taste into a fashionable mania, his

FIG. 75.—PARLOUR CHAIR. Designed by J. Mayhew.

book is by no means the first on the subject, yet most of those published were the indirect result of his youthful travels. Earlier in the century the Emperor of China's gardens had been described to assist the taste in landscape gardening, for summer-houses and rustic buildings were sometimes erected in oriental form.

As early as 1750, William Halfpenny, an unimportant architect, had issued a book of *New Designs for Chinese Temples, Triumphal Arches, Garden Seats, etc.*, for rural architecture, "the Chinese manner of building being already introduced here with success." The chairs, seats, doors, and chimney-pieces, though weak and worthless from an artistic point of view, deserve mention as showing the spread of the taste, and had probably some share in making Chambers publish his book on Chinese buildings and furniture to put "a stop to the extravagancies that daily appear under the name of Chinese, though most of them are mere inventions, and the

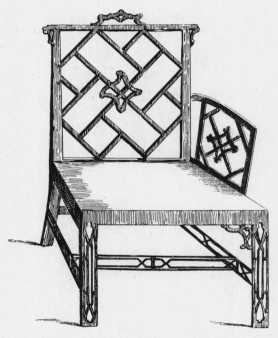

FIG. 76.—DRESSING CHAIR, Chinese style.   Designed by J. Mayhew.

rest copies from the lame representations found on porcelain and paper hangings." Another book, four years later, by Edwards and Darly, of scenes for wall decoration and plants for lacquer work, is interspersed with a few mirror-frames, brackets, candle-stands, and beds, but they are only the weakest attempt to adapt the style to English houses. The designs for frets are superior to the rest of the book, though not so varied in design as those which Crunden supplied in his series of small volumes with sentimental titles singularly inappropriate to their contents :—*The Joyner and Cabinet-maker's Darling, or Sixty Designs for Gothic, Chinese,*

Mosaic, and Ornamental Frets (1765); *The Carpenter's Companion for Chinese Railings and Gates* (in conjunction with Morris, 1770); and *The Chimney-piece Maker's Daily Assistant* (1776), which, though assisted by Milton, Overton, and Columbani, is of very inferior merit. The designers of architectural ornament, like Columbani and Mathias Darly,

FIG. 77.—A CHIMNEY-PIECE IN THE ANTIQUE MANNER.   Mathias Darly.

often deserted the higher branches of their work to render more immediate assistance to the cabinet-makers; and Darly, who was in all likelihood brought up as an architect, not only engraved Chippendale's and Ince's books, but assisted Chippendale much in the same way that Pergolesi helped Adam.

This Mathias Darly, who must not be confounded with the lesser light of the same name who collaborated with Edwards, published *A Compleat Body of Architecture, embellished with a great variety of Ornaments* (1770 and 1773). His original designs are singularly unlike what he engraved for Chippendale, the stone fireplaces alone excepted. It is possible, however, that Darly designed the two given in the *Director*, a theory borne out by the great difference between them and the general

FIG. 78.—FRAME, TO BE WORKED IN STUCCO, PAINTING, OR CARVING. Mathias Darly.

character of Chippendale's work. Darly, who calls himself a "Professor of Ornament," states that such drawing "has been too long neglected in this trading country, and great losses sustained in many of our manufactures for want of it," and absolutely claims his book to be the first publication of the kind. He exhibits great knowledge, especially of the classic styles, and, with each order illustrated, gives doors and gate-piers in accordance. Besides purely architectural matter, he also designs ceilings, panels, chimney-pieces, vases, brackets, friezes, and "frames," to be worked

FIG. 79.—MIRROR-FRAME. From Lock's "New Book of Pier Frames, Ovals, Girandoles, and Tables."

in stucco, painting, or carving. All have great classic beauty and dignity, comparing favourably with the work of other architects; but his smaller work of *Sixty Vases by English, French, and Italian Masters* (1767) is, as its title conveys, a mere selection from these styles.

When we speak of the work of the Chippendale period, most of us instinctively think of the chairs, which are so much and so justly prized.

Chippendale himself, as we have seen, shone most as a chairmaker, and it is the chairs of that epoch which are so unapproachable. But he gave almost as great prominence to his mirror designs, and it was the mirror with its carved frame which began the movement. It had long before this time been a favourite form of room decoration. In the earlier specimens the glass was cut in sheets as wide as the casting would allow, with very flat, hand-ground, and bevelled edges, cut and shaped into quaint

FIG. 80.—PIER-TABLE.   From Lock's '' New Book of Pier Frames, Ovals, Girandoles, and Tables.''

patterns, the joints sometimes covered with bands of metal or strips of coloured glass fastened by rosettes. Latterly the resources of designers and makers of decorative furniture had been reinforced by the introduction of larger plates than had been possible previously, and manufactories had been set up in France and England. This novelty gave a new departure to the designing of suitable frames, which were of carved and gilded wood, as well as painted and inlaid. Though these were largely brought over from France, still we were never without carvers in England, and the outlet provided for their work by the demand for highly ornamented mirror-frames in the houses of the wealthy raised up a number of capable craftsmen, who, when the time came for the rejuvenescence of English furniture, became the life and soul of the whole movement.

Chippendale's father is supposed to have first made his connection by this class of work, and quite a large proportion of the designers

FIG. 81.—MIRROR.   From Lock's original designs.   FIG. 82.—MIRROR.   From Lock's original designs.

whose illustrated books we possess were carvers only, and confined themselves almost entirely to frames for pictures and mirrors, or pier-table stands, on which they could display their skill.   Occasional plates of these frames had been published to begin with, singly or in sets, and some marked "H. Copeland Fecit. 16 April 1746" are still to be met with. Another carver, Matthias Lock, also made early drawings somewhere about the same time, and, though the two do not seem to have been partners in business, yet they joined together in several of the small publications which Lock issued at short intervals between 1752 and 1769. These contain ornamental designs for frames, girandoles, tables, chimney-pieces, chandeliers, and clock-cases, and were carved by Lock and his assistants "near Ye Swan, Tottenham Court Road"; for, like most of the other designers of the time, he had a workshop in which he kept a number of men to execute his own ideas to his customers' orders.   In the folio of his original drawings Lock has left interesting memoranda and rough sketches of the articles on his carving bills, with the workmen's names, prices, and other details.   From this it would appear that about

FIG. 83.—PIER-TABLE.   From Lock's original designs.

5s. per day was the average rate paid to journeymen carvers in 1742, and only 9d. and 1s. 3d. charged for "bosting" (or broad carving) two leaves or flowers, though a "brackit for a glass case with ingay figers on it for ye dresing room, over ye toilite table," amounted to £2 : 15s., as over eleven days had been spent upon it.

Lock's best work is distinguished by freedom of thought, with taste in the design as well as able execution.   A strong Italian feeling runs through it, resembling the style of Adam and others later in the century. Lock had a good eye for form, as his able studies prove.   He gives simple drawings of a plant resembling the acanthus, both treated naturally and adapted to carving, while his figure studies have great artistic feeling and power of draughtsmanship.   It was, in fact, the skill and knowledge of this class of workers which occasioned the rapid improvement in the

treatment of the heavier furniture, as well as the added delicacy and
beauty of the articles they exclusively produced.

FIG. 84.—MIRROR-FRAME. From Lock's '' New Book
of Pier Frames, Ovals, Girandoles, and Tables.''

FIG. 85.—MIRROR-FRAME.   From Lock's
original designs.

Many of Lock's original drawings are merely fragmentary hints to his
workmen, but others are finely finished. Some of his chimney-pieces in
the Louis Quatorze style are particularly good, while in others he lends
himself to the worst phases of the Chinese and Chippendale schools.

Another contemporary carver who gained considerable fame was
Thomas Johnson at the "Golden Boy," in Grafton Street, St. Ann's,
Westminster. His designs seem to have been published in parts, though
they were bound in one volume in 1758, and dedicated by an Englishman
possessing "a truly anti-Gallic spirit" to "Lord Blakeney, Grand President

FIG. 86.—CLOCK-CASE in the Chippendale style.
From Lock and Copeland's "New Book
of Ornaments."

FIG. 87.—MIRROR-FRAME.   T. Johnson.

of the laudable Association of Anti-Gallicans." Truly Johnson's ideas of
an "anti-Gallic" spirit were curious, for he considered it unpatriotic
to spend English money on the work of French hands, but highly praise-
worthy to steal French brains.

Knowing that his unsparing copies of French ornament laid him open
to a charge of duplicity from the critics, he takes the time-honoured
method of defending a bad case by abusing plaintiff's attorney. "Critics
are generally a set of people whose sole merit consists in tracing out

trivial errors, and, as Mr. Pope observes, ''twere a sin to rob them of their mite.'"

FIG. 88.—BRACKET CLOCK. T. Johnson.   FIG. 89.—TALL CLOCK-CASE. T. Johnson.

Johnson tells us that "all men vary in opinion, and a fault in the eye of one may be a beauty in that of another; 'tis a duty incumbent on an author to endeavour at pleasing every taste, and though none ever yet arrived at perfection, yet it is very evident there can be no surer road to it." So he proceeds to fulfil his aim by making his works quite little natural histories, containing almost every known and unknown specimen of animal. Flowers, birds, beasts, fishes, masks, coquillage, and scroll work are literally tossed about the frames, and theatrical representations of bears and travellers, hunting and fishing groups, appear on the table-stands in the most unnatural manner. Though to us impossible and outrageous, they were suited to the artificiality of the day, and in harmony with the flowered coats, knee breeches, diamond buckles, and double watches of the "macaroni," and the powder and patches of the belles.

Chippendale gets the credit of much of this development, and a great deal is sold under his name which really emanated from Johnson's workshop. Certainly it suggests Chippendale, but Chippendale with a touch of madness added to his most impossible designs. The fantastic cases for tall and table clocks, with figures of Time, hour-glasses, and suns' rays flashing from the summits, are more foolish and impossible than the worst of Chippendale's, and, like their French models, are altogether wanting in restraint. Some of Johnson's plainer chimney-pieces and frames must be excepted from adverse remarks, and are, like his Dolphin mantelpieces, vigorous and original. With these few exceptions, he has no merit as a designer. His curious conscience permitted him to steal his ideas unacknowledged, and his vitiated taste to spoil them in the stealing; but he was honest even in his dishonesty, and, as a carver pure and simple, helped to make English eighteenth-century furniture another name for careful and well-finished workmanship.

FIG. 90.—AN ADAM INTERIOR.

The Second Withdrawing-room in Earl Derby's house, with Sofa designed for Sir Abraham Hume, and Commode
and Glass-frame for Sir John Griffin.

V

THE BROTHERS ADAM

THE names of Robert and James Adam have come down to us as the most celebrated in the architecture of their time and country. They belonged to an architectural family, for their father, who held the office of King's Mason in Edinburgh, was well known as the designer of Hopetoun House and the old Royal Infirmary. His son John succeeded to his practice, and completed several of his unfinished buildings, and William followed the same profession, but Robert, the second son, was by far the most distinguished of the family. He was born at Kirkcaldy in 1728, educated at Edinburgh University, and at the age of twenty-two went to study in Italy, and afterwards to Dalmatia, to explore the ruins of the Emperor Diocletian's Palace at Spalatro. This work was done with great thoroughness. He took with him, not only several assistants to sketch and take measurements of the ruins, but also Clérisseau, the famous master of the still more famous Sir William Chambers.

There were great difficulties to contend against at Spalatro, as Adam was imprisoned as a spy, and his papers and drawings confiscated. But, with the indomitable energy that distinguished him in after life, he over-came all obstacles, and carried his self-imposed task through to a successful conclusion. On his return to England, he embodied the result of his labours in one large volume, dedicated to George the Third, and published in 1764. It is illustrated with the most elaborate engravings by Bartolozzi and others, after Clérisseau's and Adam's paintings, of the ruins generally, along with plans and copious explanations.

The publication of this volume contributed largely to the reputation he was beginning to make, though it gave him credit for more classic knowledge than he afterwards showed, and he rose rapidly to professional eminence, being appointed Architect to the King. This office he afterwards resigned, in order to enter Parliament, when the dignity was conferred on his brother James. In 1768, the brothers began the great undertaking in the Strand, by which they commemorated their relationship and their joint labours. They raised the Thames shore by a succession of arches, and erected a terrace and three fine streets above, fronting the river. Walpole, writing of these Adelphi buildings to Mason in 1773, speaks disparagingly of them, but his Strawberry Hill Gothic hardly gives us a high opinion of his architectural taste. Garrick, Topham Beauclerk, and other celebrities lived in this terrace. The building erected here for the Society of Arts, of which Robert Adam was a member, became the scene of many famous gatherings. Before this time, however, the whole of the Adelphi had been disposed of by a well-advertised lottery, for which the Adams had to get a special Act of Parliament. The Thames embankment scheme, which they next started, met with such popular disapproval that it had to be abandoned.

About this time (1773) the Adams began to publish engravings of their different architectural works in serial numbers, and this book has perhaps had a greater share in forming our national taste than any other. It was continued at intervals till 1778, and reached the end of a second volume, but the work was completed by the publication of a posthumous third and last in 1822. The whole is entitled the *Works in Architecture of Robert and James Adam, Esquires,* and is printed in parallel columns of French and English. It is fine both in design, execution, and taste, and, though called an architectural work, comprises as many designs for furniture as some of the actual furniture books. There are no less than sixty-four plates of mirrors, sconces, frames, slab-tables, bookcases, commodes, cabinets, chairs, lamps, clocks, organs, and door-locks, all designed to accord with the style of the interior decoration.

The bent of the Adams' style can be gathered from the symbolical frontispiece painted by Zucchi for this work, representing "a student being conducted to Minerva, who points to Greece and Italy as the countries from whence he must derive the most perfect knowledge of taste"; and they emphasise this in the preface by saying, "If we have any claims to approbation, we find it in this alone, that we flatter ourselves we have been able to seize, with some degree of success, the beautiful spirit of antiquity and transfer it with novelty and variety through all our numerous works." They declared they had "brought about, in this country, a kind of revolution in the whole system of this beautiful and elegant art," and " effected a remarkable improvement in the form, convenience, arrangement, and relief of apartments ; a greater movement and variety in the outside composition, and, in the decoration of the inside, an almost total change." Acknowledging " that nothing can be more noble and striking, when properly applied, than a fine order of columns, with their bases, capitals, and entablatures ; nothing more sterile and disgustful than to see for ever the dull repetition of Dorick, Ionick, and Corinthian entablatures reigning round every apartment, where no order can, or ought to come, and yet it is astonishing to think that this has been the case in the apartments of every house in Europe with any pretensions to magnificence, from the days of Bramante down to our time," Adam inveighed against " the massive entablature, the ponderous compartment ceiling, and the tabernacle frame," substituting his light mouldings and delicate ornaments, and imbuing both the exterior and interior with the same spirit and feeling. This led to a mannerism so distinct that one of his buildings can be distinguished at once, while the lightness and delicacy of his touch is most pleasing after the ponderosity of the preceding school.

His ideas quickly acquired the greatest popularity for room decoration and movable articles. The public were beginning to tire of the Louis Quinze style and the Chinese freaks of Chippendale and his followers, and to long for another fashion. As these extravagances had been welcomed after the severity of Queen Anne, so the tired public turned with relief to the apparently new forms which were being evolved from the ruins of ancient Greece and Rome. Eccentricity had exhausted itself by its very success, and the reaction set in. Broken scrolls were replaced by straight lines, curves and arches only appeared when justifiable, and columns and pilasters were again used for exterior and interior decoration. This revival of classic taste is sometimes attributed to the discoveries of Herculaneum and Pompeii, but these had taken place some time previously. Traces of their influence can be found in much of the decorative work of the time, but the style seems to have been welcomed for its very diversity from existing methods, more than for any popular interest taken in these discoveries.

The elegant and pretty decoration introduced by the Adams was generally well managed, though it was frequently overdone even to weakness. Festoons of drapery, wreaths of flowers caught up by rams' heads, or husks tied with knots of ribbon and oval paterae to mark a break in the design, were repeated again and again. The errors they fell into were principally want of originality and independent thought; but whatever may be the defects in the Adams' buildings, the brothers formed a style which was marked by fine sense of proportion, especially in their interiors, and by clever selection and application of cultured ornament.

It is evident that Robert Adam could design in other styles than the classic when he allowed himself to do so, both in his exteriors and interiors, for several Gothic chimney-pieces (one for Alnwick Castle) are among his original drawings. The design for one of the elaborate mantels executed for Horace Walpole is taken from the tomb of Edward the Confessor, and was carved in white marble by Richter. This, and the ceiling to match, are so unlike his usual forms, that it became a matter of speculation how much greater his success would have been had he not tied his talent down to such arbitrary standards.

The interior in our full-page illustration shows a portion of the "second withdrawing-room" in Earl Derby's house in Grosvenor Square, which was entirely after Adam's designs. "The ornaments of the pilasters, arches, and panels of the doors are beautifully painted by Zucchi. Those in the friezes of the rooms and doors are of stucco and carved wood. The magnificent glass frame in the recess is finely executed in wood and gilt." This Zucchi (Associate of the Royal Academy) rendered Adam great assistance. He accompanied him on his travels, and returned to paint the ceilings and various other portions of this building, as well as Buckingham House and Luton Hoo. Angelica Kauffmann, who afterwards married Zucchi, was also employed by Adam, and brought the warm fresh colouring and sentimental charm of her painting to grace his household decoration. Pergolesi was brought over from Italy by Adam, and to him is attributed much of the charming detail in his patron's book. The figure medallions were often his, as well as the arabesque work. The troubled condition of the Continent made foreigners glad to settle in England, and the strong Italian feeling running through Adam's designs was greatly helped by these skilful assistants, though his dominating touch is everywhere apparent. The original drawings preserved in the Soane Museum show how completely he derived his inspiration from Italy. Careful

FIG. 91.—CHIMNEY-PIECE for one of the rooms in St. James's Palace, and Steel Grate designed for Sir Watkin Wynn.   Adam.

studies of ornament and figures from the antique, Roman buildings, and fountains exist in large numbers, and the exact coloured copies made of Raphael's panels in the Vatican were used as an inspiration for much of the mural design.   His ceilings were partly in relief work and partly

FIG. 92.—PEDESTAL DECORATED WITH WEDGWOOD PLAQUE.   From South Kensington Museum.

painted, and the application of composition ornaments to woodwork was first employed for these and for the charming chimney-pieces which are about the most beautiful of the brothers' productions.   They mark a still further advance in the history of the chimney-piece, for the panels were formed of plaster and stuck on cameo-wise to the wooden framework. Adam must have taken this idea from the old "gesso" work of Italy, which had been extensively used there and in France during the fourteenth and fifteenth centuries, but was almost unknown in England. Italian artisans were naturally required to execute this plaster work, as the method of its composition was then quite unknown in this country, though it afterwards became a large industry. The analogy between this "compo" and his own processes caused Wedgwood to begin to manufacture those beautiful plaques and friezes which are now so highly prized. These he intended for furniture as well as for chimney-piece and room decoration, but he frequently deplored the lack of encouragement received. As Flaxman's classic designs blended with Adam's form, the brothers were inclined to patronise these ornaments; but the architects as a body opposed what they considered an innovation, and the taste never became really popular. Occasionally a gentleman of wealth and taste, like Sir John Wrottesley, who was not a "slave in the hands of his all-wise architect," had recourse to this style of ornament for one of his rooms. Some idea of the fine effect produced by the Wedgwood plaques united with inlay can be gathered from the satin-wood cabinet and pair of pedestals so ornamented in the South Kensington Museum.

The painstaking industry of the Adams can hardly be estimated, but the enormous number of original designs preserved in the Soane Museum conveys some slight impression of it. These are alike remarkable for clever draughtsmanship and extreme delicacy of finish; but the schemes for interior decoration are deficient in sense of tone and colour, as well as in the versatility of invention which is conspicuous in those of Sir William Chambers. The huge volumes contain not only architectural designs, but suggestions for almost everything, from articles of household use to carriages, and even sedan-chairs, one of which was designed for Queen Charlotte. Adam also decorated harpsichords after his usual manner, and even embellished their oblong cases with Wedgwood plaques; for these, as well as the newly-introduced "piano forte," followed all the mutations of fashion. Furniture alone fills up one volume, mirrors and girandoles another, while numerous furniture designs are scattered throughout the architectural pages. This furniture owed its origin wholly to Robert, and, though not actually made by the Adams, was reproduced by competent firms under their direction. Some of the designs are as poor as the others are good, but these may be mere sketches or hints for workmen; in any case, Adam did not place too high a value on them, as he left them unpublished.

Adam adapted classical forms to modern uses with a skill unrivalled by any other designer in England, for all his furniture is full of lightness and grace. The amount of decoration is never overdone, and is always

FIG. 93.—CHAIR designed by Adam for Sir A. Hume.

subordinate to the design, being only sufficient to relieve the severity of outline. Like Reisener, Adam did not show much fertility of resource in his ornament, but his designs are always well chosen and highly finished. The "gilded drawing-room chair for Sir A. Hume, in Hill Street," will show how different the form was from the bold lines of Chippendale and his followers. The designs for this chair are also interesting as showing the attention which Robert Adam always bestowed upon even the smallest detail. Separate coloured sketches are given for the pattern of the silk for the back and seat, and even the tiny cushion on the arm has a design all to itself. Adam's classic manner dominates even the smallest fittings, for he considered nothing too insignificant to come within the scope of his art. He designed the needlework, as well as the frame for the screen; the "counterpane for their Majesties," as well as the bed; and even descends to "a work-bag for Mrs. Child." This thoroughness had a great deal to do with the success of the old

Fig. 94.—An Adam Pier-table with Wedgwood Plaques.

designers both in France and England. They would never have dreamt of covering the chair of one style with the fabric belonging to another, and though this uniformity often gives a look of sameness to Adam's rooms, the monotony is more than counterbalanced by the unity of the whole. If he tied himself down to uniformity of design, he yet allowed himself considerable latitude in its expression; for though his furniture was generally gilded, yet it was frequently carved in mahogany, painted in Wedgwood colours to match the plaster walls, or inlaid in wood and stone. Alabaster or "statuary marble" was used not only for mantelpieces but for the tops of the square or round slab tables supplied to most of the interiors, indeed often to each room in the same house, and these had borders painted in Etruscan patterns, or inlaid with coloured marbles on the white ground. The sideboard tables were square in shape, and the supports of both show how Adam employed Greek ornaments pure and simple, and popularised the husk until it became almost an English decoration. The peculiar grace united to severity recalls the later French style, so much so that Adam's furniture has been rather aptly called "the English version of Louis Seize," though the source from which he derived it is too evident to allow any possibility of measurable influence from that more

FIG. 95.—TABLE IN HALL AT SHELBURNE HOUSE. Adam.

elaborate school. The sideboard tables for the Earl of Ashburnham and Lord Mansfield have separate pedestals and vases at the side, much in the style which we find later in Hepplewhite. The brass rail at the back, generally associated with Sheraton's name, as well as a great deal of the construction, shows how much Adam, though essentially an architect, had to do not only with the revival of cabinet-making, but with the development of specific articles. The classic vase in the centre, flanked by square knife-boxes, was required to break the straight lines of these table-tops, and the glittering silver ware of Adam's design helped the desired effect. Not only was the outside of these mahogany knife-boxes finely finished, but the interior was fitted up with a series of raised stages to display the carved handles or polished bowls of the spoons to the best advantage, while the lids were used as a resting-place for silver salvers.

Adam's bookcases, cabinets, and commodes are nearly all intended to be placed in recesses, for the furniture was not only planned to fit into the

Fig. 96.—Mirror for the Duke of Roxburghe.   Adam.

room, but for different positions in it.   In fact, the room was often as much devised to receive articles of furniture, as the furniture was constructed to fit its particular place.   The flat tops of the commodes were finished by a mirror, much in the style of that made for Sir John Griffin, illustrated in the principal group.   These mirrors, with or without their attendant girandoles, were beautiful pieces of workmanship, very similar to

FIG. 97.—DESIGN FOR THE STATE SIDEBOARD IN THE DINING-ROOM AT KENWOOD.   Adam.

FIG. 98.—BOOKCASE FOR LADY WYNN'S DRESSING-ROOM. Adam.

Lock's earlier designs; for all the furniture founded on classic form has naturally a strong family likeness.

FIG. 99.—GILDED TRIPOD CANDLESTAND for the Earl of Ancaster. Adam.

FIG. 100.—BRACKET AND VASE WITH BRANCHES FOR CANDLES. Adam.

A solitary instance occurs, in one of the mirror-frames, showing how Adam noticed the fast-disappearing Chinese fashion, for he placed mandarins holding classic wreaths at the top, and Chinese bells among the Italian arabesque work round the frame.   This was probably arranged to suit some room, for it never occurs in other designs.   His correct taste must have shown him how utterly impossible it was to mix the two styles satisfactorily; but it is curious to note an instance where it was again done, this time without his sanction.   Quite early in his career he built a house for Mr. Coutts

FIG. 101.—LAMP FOR ZION HOUSE. Adam.   FIG. 102.—GIRANDOLE FOR T. HOPE, ESQ. Adam.

the banker, which was afterwards hung with real Chinese paper sent over by Lord Macartney, for the fancy for Chinese paper did not die out at once. It was often used in combination with differing styles, in the same way that chairs of Chippendale construction are found decorated with lyres and wheat-ears.   Even in this century, when Abbotsford was being built, Hugh Scott of Raeburn presented some of this paper to his cousin, Sir Walter, which still exists on the drawing-room walls.

The architectural training which all the Adams received is exhibited by the special sense of proportion and fitness which the wall-lights, " terms," and tripod stands for candles evince. Their designs for metal-work were also highly successful, especially those for silver plate, and their cups, vases, candlesticks, and branches are highly valued. We are scarcely so grateful to them for the polished steel grates and fenders or the heavy window cornices which they introduced, and from which we are yet barely emancipated. The Adams' fame was so far-reaching that hardly a house or room of any pretensions was built or decorated without their plans being invited for it. They strove so earnestly to impart their spirit into

FIG. 103.—MANTELPIECE. Pergolesi.

all they undertook that they even insisted on the carpets being in unison with the surroundings, and sketched out ideas for simple-patterned borders, or elaborate Etruscan ornament like that for the drawing-room at Osterley. Horace Walpole's villa at Strawberry Hill illustrated this custom of having suitably designed carpets, for in the "Tribune" a large star in the centre of the carpet repeated that overhead in the coloured glass roof.

Not only was the Adams' great ability shown in the arrangement of these interiors, but it found wider scope in the construction and alteration of many fine public and private buildings throughout the country. They built palaces for the nobility, houses for the middle class, bridges, pavilions, theatres, churches, terraces, streets, and squares. It is impossible to

give a complete list of these, but after the Adelphi their most famous
structures are the façade of the Admiralty at Whitehall; Luton Hoo,
Bedfordshire; Shelbourne, now Lansdowne House, in Berkeley Square;
the Register House and University, Edinburgh; Keddlestone Hall, Derby-
shire; Compton Verney; Osterley, near Brentford; and Lord Mansfield's
villa of Kenwood at Hampstead.   25 Portland Place is particularly
interesting, as it was built, decorated, and finished by Robert for his
own use.   The idea of giving to a number of unimportant private houses

FIG. 104.—PANEL by Pergolesi.   FIG. 105.—PANEL by Pergolesi.

the appearance of one imposing structure originated with them, and
Portland, Stratford, and Hamilton Places are instances of how this
was effected.   The idea of using stucco for facing brick houses is another,
but more doubtful, innovation.

Robert Adam was one of the most cultivated men of his day, a
Fellow both of the Royal Society and of the Society of Arts.   The
journal of his *Tour in Italy* was printed by the Library of the Fine
Arts in 1760, and his *Vases and Foliage from the Antique* published
after his death.   He took the lead in all decorative matters, as well
as having the principal part in all the architectural undertakings shared

FIG. 106.—CEILING WITH PANEL FOR PAINTING, or to be used on furniture. Pergolesi.

by the firm. James does not appear to have possessed the same genius, but was probably overshadowed by the stronger personality of his brother. He wrote a treatise on architecture, and was engaged on a history of the same subject when he died. Though he did a certain amount of original work, he was very far behind his brother in ornamental design, and almost as far behind Michael Angelo Pergolesi, to

FIG. 107.—DOOR. From the "Modern Joiner." Wallis.

whom a considerable portion of the fame of the brothers is due. Pergolesi rendered Robert Adam immense assistance, both in internal architecture and in his books. Many of the drawings and beautiful designs in these were his, and the execution of much that he did not originate was frequently entrusted to him. It is now difficult to estimate the amount of his influence on Adam, though it is evident that it must have been great, as some of the work generally known by his employer's name can be definitely traced to his brain and hand.

Besides what he did for Adam, he published a perfect storehouse of fine Italian designs, which appeared in a series of loose numbers without letterpress, from 1777 on to the next century. Both the plaster friezes and the lighter borders for painting on furniture are naturally very like Adam's work, but the ceiling designs are more charming and varied. The doors and sides of rooms in arabesque design are particularly beautiful, and he, like his patron, introduced pier-tables, settees, and seats in harmony with the prevailing ornament. He also turned his attention to silver plate, and his serpent-wreathed jars and graceful candlesticks are the models of much modern work.

Pergolesi was particularly fond of leaving a centre in his panelled ornament to be painted either by Cipriani, Angelica Kauffmann, or

FIG. 108.—MANTELPIECE.   Columbani.

himself. The designs for these in his book, engraved by Bartolozzi, are frequently cut out and framed separately. They are mostly scenes of child life, nymphs, or amorini, and were often repeated in marquetry or painting on furniture, especially on the newly-imported satin-wood.

The Adams had many imitators among the contemporaneous architects who designed decorative items. The works of such men as W. Thomas (*Original Designs in Architecture*, 1783) lacked distinctiveness, and are practically forgotten. N. Wallis had rather more originality. He formed the ideas expressed in his *Book of Ornament in the Palmyrene Taste* (1771) entirely on Greek lines, and helped the fittings of the house by giving good chimney-pieces, doorcases with their mouldings, friezes, tablets, and cornices, in his *Modern Joiner* (1772).

Columbani's books—*Vases and Tripods* (1770), *A New Book of Ornament* (1775), and *A Variety of Capitals, Friezes, Corniches* (sic), *and how*

to increase and decrease them, still retaining their proportions (1776)—
contain good panel designs for painting and stucco, and excellent chimney-
pieces, all strongly resembling, and almost equal to, the productions of Adam

FIG. 109.—WALL-PANEL, TO BE EXECUTED IN WOOD, STUCCO, OR PAINTING. Columbani.

and Richardson. The chimney-pieces of all the later eighteenth-century
architects were of strongly pronounced Italian character. Whether carved
in stone or wood, painted, or cast in stucco, they formed one of the
greatest ornaments of the rooms, and agreed in style with the mural
decoration. Those which George Richardson published in his *Collection*

of Chimney-pieces ornamented in the Style of the Etruscan, Greek, and Roman Architecture (1781) were to be carried out in various ways, among which was the free use of different coloured marbles. The side columns were often made of scagliola, or the flutings variegated to suit the colour of the room. Then again the ornament was often painted on wood or marble, sometimes in natural colours, but oftener in the fashion of Etruscan work, or in "chiaroscuro" (by which he means absence of colour) "on a dark ground." Many of these mantelpieces are so similar to those of Adam that they might be mistaken for the work of the architect whom he endeavoured to rival. His influence on wall decoration during the later part of the century is only second to that of the Adams, and his *Book of Ceilings in the Style of the Antique Grotesque* (1776) has a great resemblance to the brothers' volume, challenging comparison with it. It breathes the same spirit of scholarly culture and refinement, with almost the same creative power. Probably to emphasise the difference between his drawings and those of the brothers, he disowns any classic origin for them, though they run on very similar lines. The centre pictures in the ceilings represent scenes from Greek mythology or Roman history, and bacchanalian figures or nymphs decorate the corners. In the series of rooms executed for Sir Laurence Dundas, the drawing-room is decorated with nymphs sacrificing to Hymen, the dining-room with a feast of the gods attended by Ganymede and Hebe, the ante-room has nymphs sacrificing to Terminus, the supper-room represents the feast of Antony and Cleopatra, while the hall and vestibule have similarly suitable panels. Many examples of his work may be met with all over the country, for he was largely employed in interior decorations. He designed a ceiling in the Grecian hall at Keddleston, and his fine mantels and ceilings form the principal attraction to many of the houses built about this time.

Richardson's scholarly attainments were great, and his publications many. *New Designs in Architecture* (1792) shows sections of rooms with panelled recesses, columns, and friezes to be worked out in composition or "painted in colours to suit rooms hung with figured silk or paper." *Original Designs for Country Seats or Villas* (1795) gives similar stucco ornaments to those of Adam, with slightly more variety and freedom. These, with *Ædes Pembrochianæ*, a description of antiquities and curiosities at Wilton House (1798), and the new *Vitruvius Britannicus* (1802-1808), are but a few of his publications, which ran on to 1816.

FIG. 110.—CHIMNEY-PIECE, WITH TABLET REPRESENTING THE TRIUMPH OF VENUS.

"The plain grounds round the pilasters with Termes may be of variegated colour, but all the rest of pure white marble." Richardson.

FIG. 111.—SHEARER FURNITURE, WITH HEPPLEWHITE MIRROR AND CHAIR OF THE PERIOD.

VI

THOMAS SHEARER AND THE SOCIETY OF LONDON CABINET-MAKERS' BOOK OF PRICES

THE London Cabinet-makers existing between 1770 and the end of the century devoted their best energies to improving the furniture of the time, but, except in a few solitary instances where they possessed some distinguishing mark, or were enabled to publish for themselves, their names are altogether forgotten. This was as much the case in the Adams' era as it had been twenty years before, and the long list of cabinet and chair makers, carvers, upholsterers, and other kindred tradesmen in Sheraton's book in 1793 proves how many well-known and established businesses must have been in existence for a long time previously. Adam's furniture had been made by Gillow and other early firms, under his personal superintendence, and most of the cabinet-makers followed more or less the same classic manner.

The group included in the above Society broke quite new ground in their *Cabinet-makers' Book of Prices* (1788), for in it the working cost of the various articles of furniture are given for the first time. Though Chippendale's and other catalogues were as much for the "gentleman" as the "cabinet-maker," this was provided more for the worker than the customer, and was printed for the Society and sold at the "White Swan" in Shoe Lane, the "Marquis of Granby" in Oxford Market, and at the "Unicorn," corner of Henrietta Street, Covent Garden. The price of any piece of work can, we are told, "be easily found, for which reason there are no plates of the common work, that being what any one may settle without the assistance of a drawing."

The frontispiece may be safely described as the only piece of flourish or conceit in the whole; for the short, practical tone is a pleasing contrast to the flowery descriptions and classical invocations in the preface of every similar work.   Cupid, with square and compasses comfortably tucked under his arm, offers a scroll inscribed "Unanimity with Justice" to a classically attired lady, leaning against a pillar, while a bureau book-case stands in the background in an endeavour to render the idea a little more appropriate.   The members of the Society certainly possessed unanimity of aim, but justice they have hardly received, for, among them all, Hepplewhite alone has met with a fair amount of recognition.   At the time the Society was formed, Shearer and the others were probably regarded quite as much as the introducers of what we consider Hepplewhite furniture as A. Hepplewhite and Co. themselves.

The book was evidently intended more as a publication for the trade

FIG. 112.—SERPENTINE DRESSING-CHEST WITH OGEE ENDS.   Shearer.

FIG. 113.—SERPENTINE DRESSING-CHEST WITH STRAIGHT WINGS.   Shearer.

than for the general public, for short and sensible directions to working cabinet-makers introduce the two hundred descriptions and twenty-nine copperplates.   In the second edition, published in 1793, they say, "Many articles in the first edition not being clear enough to prevent different constructions being put on them by journeymen and their employers, as their different interests might suggest, (which has been the cause of frequent and in some cases irreconcilable disputes between them,) in order, therefore, to prevent as much as possible the like evil occurring in future, it is requested that both parties will be particular in making themselves acquainted with the following general directions."

From this it would appear that the intention of the book was to furnish fair prices between master and man for piecework, which had superseded the day-work of a previous generation.   The quotations must not be taken as more than a rough guide to the ultimate cost of the finished article as supplied to the customer.   This was probably much higher, as not

FIG. 114.—FRENCH COMMODE DRESSING-CHEST.   Shearer.

only had the master's profit to be added, but also the cost of materials, rent, etc., which would come to at least as much again.

Ambiguity is confined entirely to the frontispiece, for it would be almost impossible for even the most obtuse journeyman carpenter to miscalculate the charges.   The smallest items are carefully provided for,

FIG. 115.—CONTENTS OF A "FURNITURE DRAWER."   Society of Cabinet-makers.

and the book was of such value to the master cabinet-maker of the time, that men still living can remember its being in general use.   A sample of the workman's charges for extras in a "furniture drawer" will be of interest, as showing the almost amusingly minute particulars the Cabinet-makers' Society went into :—

	s.	d.
Each square hole formed by partitions the depth of the drawer .	0	3½
Each partition for rings, combs, etc., that are shallow . .	0	2
A glass frame hinged to sliding piece	4	0
A horse behind ditto	0	1
Framing the sliding piece	0	4
A frame for the glass to fall into	1	4
Making the glass frame, or piece the frame is hinged to, fit a sweep front	0	4
A straight front drawer under the glass	1	0
A sweep front ditto	1	6
A drawer in the end for ink, sand, and wafers . . .	3	0
A hollow for pins or pens	0	4
Each square loose cover	0	4
Each square to fit a sweep front	0	6
Rounding or champhering each cover	0	3
Veneering each cover	0	1
Hinging each cover	0	3
Putting a lock on ditto	0	3½
Putting thin stuff inside holes to form a rabbit for cover, each side	0	1
Each square box without a top	0	1
Each box to fit the sweep of front	0	2
(Prices of covers to ditto same as above)		
Rabbiting the top, and fixing one part fast the other part hinged to ditto	0	8
A square box with top cut off and a rim inside ditto . .	1	8
Ditto to fit a sweep front	2	8
An empty lift-out	0	9
Each hole in ditto formed by partition	0	2
Each false bottom under rings, combs, or lift-out . .	0	2
If made to tilt	0	4
A plain comb tray	1	3
Each finger hole in ditto	0	1
Scalloping the edges	0	4
Rabbiting the bottom on ditto	0	3
If made with a drawer to ditto	3	0
A square pin-cushion board with a moulding round ditto .	0	6
A frame for ditto	0	10
An oval ditto and preparations	2	0
A square brush top	0	6
An oval brush top and preparations	2	0
A plain slider, square clamped	2	6
A flap to ditto	1	0
A horse to ditto	0	10
A bottom under ditto	0	6
Hanging the flaps with a bead and band round ditto . .	0	9

	s.	d.
Making the slides to fit the inside of round front . .	0	4
Ditto serpentine	0	6
Lining the slider with cloth	0	9
Ditto when a flap	1	0
Lopers to support drawer	4	0
Lining inside of drawer with bead stuff	0	8
Ditto when round front	0	10
Ditto when serpentine	1	0
Every inch above 3 feet in length of drawer . . .	0	2

Fig. 116.—Curious Wash-stand with an imitation Wedgwood Vase, opening in the centre.
Belonging to Sir W. Welby Gregory.

Secret drawers or compartments were quite a feature in the cabinets, secretaires, and writing-tables of the period. In the days when banks were few and people kept valuables in their own custody, they were used as a safe hiding-place for money or deeds. Sir Joshua Reynolds's plain mahogany cash-box, lately sold at Christie's, contained secret drawers not only in the bottom, but also in the sides and lid.

Another class of furniture very typical of the times is shown in the many ingenious devices for folding furniture. The demand for these must have been very great in an age when the bedroom became, during the day, a sitting and even a reception room. To such lengths were the purposes of concealment carried that a folding wash-stand of this period in the possession of Sir W. Welby Gregory has a vase on the top carved in wood and coloured to imitate Wedgwood ware, which opened in the centre when the table was required for toilet purposes.

Folding bedsteads were necessarily among the commonest pieces of furniture required for these rooms. Field and tent bedsteads are given in

FIG. 117.—OLD HEPPLEWHITE WINE-TABLE. From London Cabinet-makers' Book of Prices.

the *Director* as well as in other books of the time, but the Society supply a still fuller list. They not only made "press" and "library press" bedsteads, but caused ordinary tables, toilet-tables, and bureaux to conceal wooden frames and mattresses. No illustration is given of the ingenious way in which these beds were hidden in their disguise. They have been consigned to the limbo of departed things with Hepplewhite's gouty stool and Sheraton's chamber-horse, but several other pieces alluded to in the book still exist in old inns and well-preserved houses.

The wine-table still surviving in some of the Colleges of Oxford and Cambridge is here delicately termed a "Gentleman's Social Table," and the Society provided for "extra bottle-cases" being cut in the revolving top.   Varieties of these tables are still to be found in a few old country houses, as well as in the Charterhouse.   In the later Sheraton period they frequently received further conveniences, and were decorated with brass inlay and carving.   The form is invariably a half circle or horse-shoe, having a loose or portable centre, which, when removed, discloses a net to

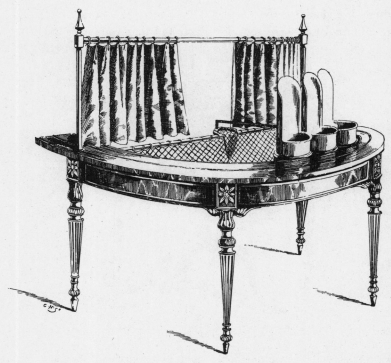

FIG. 118.—INLAID WINE-TABLE OF THE SHERATON PERIOD, WITH CURTAIN-RAIL, NET, AND WINE-CARRIAGE.

hold biscuits, or, possibly, to catch the glasses when upset by the too convivial gentlemen.   Round the outer circumference the guests were seated, and the wine-carriage, balanced by a weight, travelled round the inner side.   The mahogany bottle-cases were provided with high metal or wooden shields to keep the heat of the fire from the wine, for the ends of this make of table folded up to allow of its being pushed against the sides of the mantelpiece.   Many of the backs are provided with a running curtain, so that, should the heat become too great, there would still be no necessity for removing either the table or the gentlemen. When the wine-cases required replenishing, the Society's bottle-trays with partitions "cut to receive the necks of the bottles," the square or hexagon bottle-carriers "to hold four wine-bottles upright," and the brass-hooped wine-pails came into requisition, for these were the days when too often a man's highest distinction was to be known as a "three-bottle man," and that not of the light wine which the French wars had prohibited, but of the heavier vintages of Spain and Portugal.

With practical foresight, the Society provided little folding or upright "dispensaries" to stand on brackets against the bedroom wall; and these, with their medicine cases replaced by drawers, are nowadays turned into

FIG. 119.—SHERATON'S "GRECIAN DINING-TABLE."

jewel cabinets. "Cylinder netting-cases" have long been obsolete, but the dumb-waiter, plate-carrier, and table book-stand mentioned bring us to our own times, and are still in common use.

Prices are given for the different shapes of dining-tables then in vogue. The cabinet-makers mention several varieties of the "flap" and "pillar and claw" shapes which had superseded the many-legged oak gate or "drawinge" tables of previous centuries. Ever since its introduction, mahogany had been pre-eminently the wood employed for these tables, but about this time bands and lines of inlay were sometimes added.

The square or oval flap-top was supported by legs which folded into the side when not in use, like the "dining-table with one or two flaps, hung with rule or square joints, four plain Marlborough legs, and one fly on each side." These tables served by themselves for family use, but when it was necessary to seat a larger number they were placed in the centre, and "half-moon" ends of similar construction added, which, when separate, were suitable either for side-tables or folded into small space against the wall.

The horse-shoe shapes which the Society mentions are very little known. They also had flaps, and "plain taper legs with the flaps supported either way." The guests were seated round the outer side, and served from the other. Occasionally a dumb-waiter was placed in the centre, either for the servants' use, or in order to dispense with them altogether, and this idea was adopted by Sheraton in his later "Grecian Table" of the same shape.

FIG. 120.—LADY'S CABINET WORK-TABLE.   By Hepplewhite.

This was made in three pieces, with flaps joined together with brass fasteners on the under side, like those in the Court Room of the Skinners' Company; but the earlier horse-shoe table of the time of the Cabinet-makers' Society seems to have been made in one, with the extended flaps, supported on underframing, to form the horse-shoe.

"Pillar and claw" tables are much more common. These were constructed with a central leg fixed into a block at the top and bottom. The top was hinged to the upper block, and the three legs, which were fastened to the lower, generally ended in the castored claws that gave their name to the whole. They were of various forms, and Sheraton made a circular kind with a double top, the upper part revolving like the shelves

of the dumb-waiter in the centre.   An extension could also be made for
these tables, when square in shape, by placing several together, though it
could hardly have been a steady arrangement.   Nothing better was devised
till about 1800, when Gillow distanced other competitors by patenting
telescope slides "as an improvement in the method of constructing dining

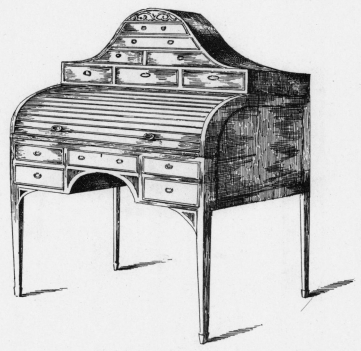

FIG. 121.—CYLINDER WRITING-TABLE, WITH ARCHED TOP CONTAINING NEST
OF DRAWERS.   Shearer.

and other tables, calculated to reduce the number of legs, pillars, and
claws, and to facilitate and render easy their enlargement and reduction."

An interesting list of the woods employed is given in the Book of Prices,
of which the most important is the mention of satin-wood, "either solid
or veneered."   This would seem to militate against the generally received
opinion that no article was manufactured entirely of satin-wood until later
in the century.   Among the other woods are manilla, safisco, havannah,
king, tulip, rose, purple, snake, zebra, alexandria, panella, yew, and maple,
which were generally employed for inlay and marquetry.

The Cabinet-makers' Society may have had many members, but three only appear to have designed the plates.   These were Shearer, Hepplewhite, and Casement.   Shearer was responsible for the largest share of the work, twenty pages bearing his signature.   Hepplewhite produced seven, and William Casement, of whom there is no other mention, filled two with

FIG. 122.—CYLINDER WRITING AND TOILET TABLE COMBINED.   Shearer.

beautiful metal-work panels for bookcase fronts.   As Chippendale belonged to the Society of Upholsterers, so Hepplewhite appears to have been associated with the Cabinet-makers, publishing his own book about the same time without severing his connection.   The cost of making a great many of his peculiar pieces of furniture, such as urn-tables (4s. 3d. to 8s.) and tripod flower-stands (5s.), was given without illustrations being supplied.   His designs include the wine-table already alluded to, and a reading-desk and

toilet-table which do not merit any particular mention. A gentleman's
writing-table and lady's cabinet work-table have more resemblance to the
contemporaneous work of Sheraton than any of the designs in Hepplewhite's
book. A kidney table is also almost identical with Sheraton's, down to the
reading-desk on the top.

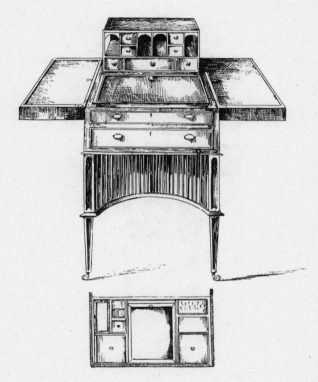

FIG. 123.—HARLEQUIN TABLE, WITH CONTENTS OF FLAP TOP. Shearer.

A graceful cabinet bookcase, with eagle top and panels of painted nymphs,
evinces Hepplewhite's desire to follow " the newest taste," lest the fate
which Sheraton predicted should descend; but his pages of standards for
fire-screens, " therms " for claws, and mouldings are much more distinctive
of the man.

It is not clear whether the designs of Thomas Shearer were published
separately or not, as the twenty pages marked "Shearer delin. published
according to act of parliament 1787 " are bound up without title page or

description.   He was one of the working cabinet-makers of the time, and produced much excellent furniture.   In all likelihood he and Hepplewhite were friends as well as fellow-workers, though it is easy to see that Shearer had less education and artistic feeling.   His furniture is apt to be heavy, like the large bookcase with secretaire front sketched in the group.   The doors have the well-designed metal-work which is quite a feature in the productions of all the members of the Society, and, like much other furniture of the time, brings in the Prince of Wales feathers again and again.   His knee-hole writing-table is only differentiated by its serpentine front from

FIG. 124.—SHAVING-TABLE.   Shearer.

the modern office-table ; but he tried to introduce the ogee line wherever possible, as the illustrations of dressing chests and drawers prove.

No deficiency of grace or lightness can be charged against the two cylinder writing-tables (Figs. 121 and 122), almost alike in shape, except for the arched top on the one, and shield-shaped glass finishing the other. Some tambour-topped tables are still more intricate, the inside pulling out and making tray slides for writing or working, while places for papers are arranged within ; for Shearer positively revels in making the outside of his articles quite unlike their inside use.   They serve both purposes equally well, as the practical bearing is kept in mind.   Economy of space was another peculiarity, and he suggested interior fittings for bureaux, drawers,

and compartments on nearly every page.   A magical table rightly called
" Harlequin " has a sliding nest of drawers or " till " which can be raised
to any height by means of intricate machinery.   When enclosed in the
table it is held so securely by catches that, were the whole turned upside
down, it would still keep its place.   Sheraton took the plan of this for his
harlequin pembroke table, for which he assumes " very little originality or
merit, the rest being due to a friend from whom I received my first ideas
of it."   Shearer, not content with this exhibition of mechanical power,

FIG. 125.—LADY'S DRESSING-TABLE, WITH ADJUSTABLE MIRRORS.   Shearer.

makes the table still more like an article from the Arabian Nights.   When
the flap top is pulled up, a folding glass and toilet compartments appear.
Every detail is given in the drawing, down to the " pincushion board with a
moulding " in which the pins are faithfully depicted, Shearer being nothing
if not realistic.   We tremble to think of the extras for this table, as every
fresh hiding-place must have piled on a little more.

The Rudd, or Lady's Dressing table has nothing to distinguish it from
Hepplewhite's, but the £2 : 3s. charged seems very little indeed for such
complicated mechanism, though that does not include the work inside the
"furniture drawers."   The toilet-tables and wash-stands are of the same

multum in parvo description, opening out in all directions with fresh surprising-places for dressing apparatus.   One, hardly more elaborate than the

FIG. 126.—CIRCULAR CELLARET SIDEBOARD.   Shearer.

rest, has folding mirrors which can be adjusted at any angle to reflect the person seated before them, but which fold under the top so cleverly that

FIG. 127.—SIDEBOARD WITH ELLIPTIC MIDDLE AND OGEE ON EACH SIDE.   Shearer.

the table presents no unusual appearance when closed.   Even the little corner wash-stands we are all familiar with have in many cases shaving-glasses behind or folding tops and sides.

The grand design in the book is the sideboard with circular front and

pedestal sides (Fig. 111), which has more the appearance of the early
Victorian than the Georgian era.   The doors have figures of nymphs
and children, evidently intended for inlay, and a group of fruit is represented on the back.   The effect of the whole is so heavy that even the
delicate knife-boxes can do little to lighten it.   Though more ambitious,
it is not equal in grace to his cellarette sideboards, particularly that
"with an elliptic middle and ogee on each side."

Towards the end of the book we come to uncommon designs for little

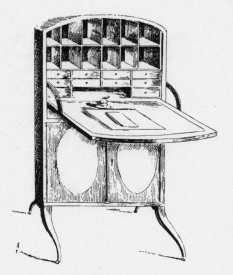

FIG. 128.—WRITING FIRE-SCREEN.   Shearer.

"writing fire-screens," which exist in the work of no other cabinet-maker.
The falling shelf allows the screen to be used for writing close to a fire
without any inconvenience from the heat.   For the same purpose Sheraton
added a sliding screen to an ordinary table, but Shearer's are more
portable, and the pigeon-holes and drawers, not to mention the cupboards,
give more accommodation than the depth would at first seem to permit.
These appear to have been made both in mahogany and satin-wood, inlaid
or painted, but are surprisingly rare considering their lightness and utility.

Two curious facts strike us as regards this book.   In the first place,
there is no attempt at any description or explanation of the articles;
secondly, there is not a single illustration of a chair.   A possible, though

not altogether likely, reason for this may have been the wish on the part of Shearer not to trench on Hepplewhite's ground.

Shearer was not a man of much education, for, had he possessed learning, he could hardly have failed to exhibit it in the bombastic time to which he belonged. Claiming no high inspiration, he kept to his aim of providing good solid furniture for everyday people, which, though never rising to the highest beauty of which the style is capable, is yet singularly devoid of the least attempt at show or ostentation. All the ornament is simple and easily carried out, and, though not very original in character, shows a feeling above that of a common workman. We know nothing of him as a man, save that he lived and worked and died, but he must have been hard-working to have acquired his practical knowledge; ingenious, to have devised his elaborate detail; sensible, not to overload his structures with purposeless ornament; and solid-headed, not to be carried away at a time when the French style was being slavishly imitated by men he must have recognised as his artistic superiors.

VII

A. HEPPLEWHITE[1]

HEPPLEWHITE does more than merely stand out from the many minor authors who, during the latter part of the eighteenth century, kept up an unbroken flow of more or less original design. His book of three hundred articles of furniture is one of the most important contributions to English cabinet-making. He lacked the power of invention and exquisite sense of proportion which are so fully displayed in Chippendale's work, and, compared with Sheraton, there is a certain weakness in his arrangement of ornament. But, on the other hand, he possesses lightness combined with unassuming grace, and withal a thoroughly English bias. It is for these reasons that he is more of a living power to-day in his influence on our modern furniture than any other of the great group of eighteenth-century cabinet-makers, Chippendale himself not excepted.

Just as his designs are less cumbrous than those of the school which was rapidly disappearing, so is his volume less pedantic and more graceful. Yet he styles the heavier furniture of Chippendale, Mayhew, and Manwaring " the productions of whim at the instance of caprice," and he prides himself on omitting " such things whose recommendation was mere novelty, and perhaps a violation of all established rule," while he states his own general object to be " to unite elegance with utility, and blend the useful with the agreeable."

Alas for the futility of time and fashion! Hepplewhite's own book was criticised some five years later by Sheraton as having usefulness only for a time, and serving to show the change from the taste of former ages when the fashion had become obsolete ; in fact, merely of antiquarian value.

[1] The name seems to have been spelt in two ways : Heppelwhite in the first edition, and Hepplewhite in the third. Both spellings are used indifferently on the plates in the Cabinet-makers' Book of Prices, though Sheraton, in his preface, adheres to the earlier form.

FIG. 129.—A HEPPLEWHITE DRAWING-ROOM.

Perhaps it is as well for Sheraton's peace of mind that he could not look forward a hundred years and see, that instead of this style " catching the decline and dying suddenly of the disorder," ten of our modern chairs now owe their existence to Hepplewhite for every one that takes its inspiration from him.

The *Cabinet-maker and Upholsterer's Guide*, from drawings by A. Hepplewhite and Co. (1788 and 1789), seems to have been the work of a firm of several men, and Hepplewhite's connection with the Cabinet-makers' Society would suggest the possibility that he, Shearer, and several others, though they had their own separate shops, may have worked more or less together in design. The book of prices in which they all joined, and Shearer's own volume, were published about the same time as Hepplewhite's, but they are all so much alike that the probability of their having a considerable share in each other's work is strengthened, especially since Shearer omits all mention of seats as if he wished to give his associates greater scope.

Hepplewhite seems to have been better educated than Shearer, and more able to express his intentions elegantly. Whatever he manufactured was practical, and thoroughly English in intention, though the ornamental additions to the structural design were, in many cases, borrowed from the classic form of Louis Seize.

The Chinese style of Chambers had been superseded by the influence of the brothers Adam. Houses were almost entirely built in the classic style, and the interiors decorated with festoons of drapery, wreaths of flowers caught up by rams' heads, and lines of husks terminating in knots of ribbon. Other architects were following in the same manner, and the walls and ceilings were being painted by Pergolesi, Cipriani, and Angelica Kauffmann, whose panels of nymphs, goddesses, or amorini were surrounded by arabesque work. Furniture with a similar style of decoration was required for these changed conditions, and Hepplewhite supplied the demand. The same artists who painted the ceilings and walls, as well as Catton and Baker, helped to ornament the articles Hepplewhite manufactured, and the coach-painters, whose employment was gradually leaving them, were glad to assist with this congenial work. Elegant medallions, in addition to inlay, were placed upon chairs, table centres, harpsichord cases, and commodes. Mahogany was largely embellished in this manner, but satin-wood, which had just been introduced from the East Indies, was a still more favourite ground-work for decoration. Mantelpieces, hitherto confined to the sculptor's art, now had wreaths of flowers beautifully painted in on the natural wood, with plaques in grisaille or colours, and even marble often received its chief decoration in this way. Light and fantastic elegance became the fashion, plain wood being discarded for coloured enrichments, and these artistic trifles gave quite a different aspect to English rooms.

In common with the best designers of the eighteenth century,

FIG. 130.—HEPPLEWHITE CARD-TABLE in Satin-wood.

Hepplewhite possessed a breadth of view and a love of art for art's sake which removed him from the position of a mechanic and tradesman to that of a patriotic artist whose wish to improve his art was as great as his desire to benefit pecuniarily by it. He not only tells us that his "judgment was called forth in selecting such patterns as were most likely to be of general use, in choosing such points of view as would show them most distinctly, and in exhibiting such fashions as were necessary to answer the end proposed, and convey a just idea of England's taste in furniture for houses," but he goes a step further and adds that he was anxious to give the benefit of his improvements to "our own countrymen and artisans whose distance from the metropolis makes even an imperfect knowledge of its improvements acquired with much trouble and expense." This open-mindedness was very greatly the cause of the eighteenth-century move-

FIG. 131.—POLE FIRE-SCREEN. Hepplewhite.

ment being so widespread and successful. The best designs were published freely, without any desire on the part of the designer to reserve any benefit accruing from them to himself, hence the working cabinet-makers throughout the kingdom copied the designs in every way, sometimes succeeding in imparting to their work as much refinement and dignity as was expressed in the original, but in many other cases falling far short of the conception.

The form of the chair back is one of the distinguishing marks between the three great cabinet-makers. The shield or heart-shaped back was Hepplewhite's hall-mark, and, whether the legs were straight or curved, the outline of the back remained the same, though in a few instances a square or a plain oval was resorted to. His chairs were smaller than Chippendale's, chiefly in entire height and width of seat, for dress

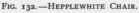

FIG. 132.—HEPPLEWHITE CHAIR.   FIG. 133.—HEPPLEWHITE CHAIR.

had come down to the scantier proportions which these could easily accommodate. The square legs which Chippendale adopted from the Chinese are tapered and thinned down by Hepplewhite till they appear almost unable to support even the diminished seat. He, however, cleverly combines a look of fragility with a fair amount of strength by turning out the lower part of the leg, or by using the "spade foot," as the square excrescence at the thin end of the leg is called. Here the eye instinctively produces the lines of the rapidly tapering leg, and, in spite of the strong end, we mentally take them to be the real lines of the leg. This is simply an optical illusion with a purpose. From first to last his work was a protest against the heaviness of Chippendale's, and he used every means in his power to make his furniture look even lighter than it was.

On the backs of his chairs Hepplewhite spent much time and thought. Yet when we compare his book with either Chippendale's or Sheraton's in this respect we can hardly help a feeling of disappointment that so few of his designs are worthy of comparison with theirs. But his best work

FIG. 134.—HEPPLEWHITE CHAIR.

is of such very great excellence that he well deserves the high place universally accorded to him. His "banister" backed chairs are very distinctive, and for these he gives eighteen designs evidently intended to be carried out in mahogany. He tells us that "the bars and frames of the chairs are made sunk in a hollow, or rising in a round projection, with a band or lift on the inner and outer edges; many of these are enriched with ornament proper to be carved." Drapery is generally to be met with in the shield, as well as urns, husks, flowers, and ribbons for splats and banisters.　He popularised the wheat-ear or inverted bell-flower till it became almost as well known as Chippendale's ribbon back or Sheraton's lyre.

Hepplewhite had yet another speciality.　This was "a very elegant fashion which had arisen of late years of finishing them (chair backs) with painted or japanned work, which gives a rich and splendid appearance to the minuter parts of the ornaments, which are generally thrown in by

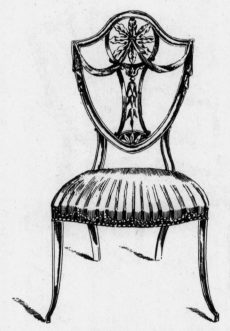

FIG. 135.—CARVED CHAIR.　Hepplewhite.

the painter."　Japanning was, however, no novelty in England, though perhaps never applied in this way to chairs.　The fashion for Chinese lacquer work had been imported from the East long before, and both Chinese examples and their Dutch copies were well known; for "commodes of old Japan," and "Japan cabinets, Indian and English," constantly appear in old lists and advertisements.　Pieces of furniture used to be sent out to China in the tea-ships to be coated with lacquer, till the English craftsmen began to imitate it for themselves.　Though these first attempts had been gradually improved on, and the art fostered by Chambers's Chinese taste, yet it had never reached the state of perfection to which it was brought by the Martin family in Paris about the middle of the century. By them the ornaments under the varnish were not confined to Japanese and Chinese subjects, but mythological scenes, *fêtes champêtres*, flower borders, and heraldic ornament were added. Hepplewhite derived his speciality from this source, as his chairs were

FIG. 136.—JAPANNED OR PAINTED CHAIR. Hepplewhite.

coated with a preparation of lacquer, and then generally painted with gold on a black ground, in designs of fruit or flowers enclosing monochrome ovals of figures. This modern japanning soon became a most favourite mode of decoration in all sorts of furniture, and was largely imitated in amateur work, like the cabinet "japanned by Lady Walpole" mentioned in the *Description* from the Strawberry Hill press. Though very popular at the time, the style had only a short reign; white grounds were substituted, till the whole degenerated into the white and burnished gold of Sheraton's French chairs.

When Hepplewhite wrote that a framework less massy than is used for mahogany should be employed for these chairs, he referred to the appearance more than the material, and suggested that by arranging the colour of the grounds to be employed to suit the room, it would have a still more pleasing and striking effect. No doubt it had this appearance when new, but, in the specimens which have descended to us, little of the original grandeur has survived. The carving on the shield backs and wheat-ears is as good as ever; but the gold, paint, and varnish have in most cases been swept away by the hand of time, or, what is even worse, "re-touched" by the hand of the vandal "restorer" till all the beauty of the original is lost.

Hepplewhite's chairs were mainly designed for the room then known as the "parlour," which would seem, to our modern ideas, rather a waste of good material. But the word has changed its signification several times, and Hepplewhite did not mean what we do by its use. Parlours are first heard of in mediæval times, when they were a part of the common hall, screened off as a place of retirement for the family. They gradually became a separate room, sometimes partaking of the character of a bedroom, and were used to sup in, while dinner was still served in the large hall. Later, the term came to be employed as a synonym for our modern "dining-room"; for we learn from Johnson in 1755 that it was "a room on the first floor, elegantly furnished, for reception or entertainment," and from Bailey, at a later date, that its purpose was "for receiving company." Sheraton and Hepplewhite used the words "parlour" and "dining-room" as convertible terms, and so they remained for some time, till they each acquired a more modern and restricted signification. The seats of the chairs for this room were covered with horsehair cloth—not the black, hideous stuff we associate with the name, but in coloured, striped, or raised chequered designs, the edges being finished off with rows of closely studded nails.

In Plate IX. of the first edition of Hepplewhite's book there are two designs for chairs with cane seats, the backs of both being rectilinear and ungraceful. Though cane had been used in chairs earlier in the century, it had fallen into disuse, and Hepplewhite and Sheraton did much to render it again popular, and, finely executed, it was applied to the backs and sides of beds, settees, and other furniture.

He applies the name "cabriole" to the stuffed-back chair, which Chippendale and other writers termed "French." He does not seem, as we do, to mean any particular shape of leg thereby, for only one of the chairs has a "cabriole" support, and he merely remarks regarding it, "To this design we have given a French foot." These stuffed chairs were apparently the newest fashion, and were "executed with good effect for His Royal Highness the Prince of Wales."

Hepplewhite was one of the Prince's party, and a convincing proof of his loyalty to his patron may be found in the frequent occurrence of the Royal plume within the shield back, or crowning the tops of other pieces

FIG. 137.—CABRIOLE CHAIR. Hepplewhite.

FIG. 138.—CABRIOLE CHAIR WITH FRENCH FOOT. Hepplewhite.

of furniture. The popularity of the Prince's party when the illness of George the Third caused such strife, may be guessed from the large number of feather chairs still to be met with.

Hepplewhite's "state chairs" have also stuffed backs with curvilinear legs. The framework was intended to be japanned with burnished gold ornaments on a dark ground, and the seats to be covered with red morocco.

Easy-chairs appear to have been part of the bedroom furniture of wealthy people all through the eighteenth century. These were some-times covered with the same stuff as the bed and window curtains.

Hepplewhite calls these easy-chairs "saddle-check," but the general name seems to have been "wing" or "forty wink."

Seats of all kinds occupied Hepplewhite's attention, and not only was he successful in designing pretty and comfortable chairs, but he was quite as much so in constructing the other pieces of furniture of similar use which were required for the reception-rooms of the day.

Sofas had always been favourite pieces of eighteenth-century furniture,

FIG. 139.—EASY-CHAIR.　Hepplewhite.

and all sorts of designs for them were given in the books of the various cabinet-makers.　From many of these one might gather that the sofa developed, not from the bare bench of the Middle Ages, as some writers assert, but from the bed.　The relationship between bed and sofa was, at all events, very close; for in old examples there may be seen a mattress, and even pillows, while Chippendale designed a canopied reclining place, and entitled it a "sofa-bed."　During the latter part of the century it seems to have evolved in two directions—the settee, and the sofa proper.　The settee was sometimes made in the form of two or more chair-backs with arms at the end, the backs being pierced wood, or a framing of bars in a fancy shape, either in mahogany or satin-wood, frequently painted after the style of Vernis-Martin work to match the other furniture in the room. The sofa took an independent course, and became more and more Classic, till it ended in the "Grecian" sofa of Sheraton's later furniture. Hepplewhite gives five designs for stuffed-back sofas. Though the temptation to stick on some ornamental excrescence is not to be resisted, yet he endeavours to afford an easy and comfortable lounge. There are, however, too many unnecessary curves in the back—intended to give grace, but merely suggesting weakness. It is evident, from some of these designs, that

FIG. 140.—BAR-BACK SOFA. Hepplewhite.

cabriole legs were still being made to suit public taste; but the coming change in favour of straight supports, which Sheraton developed with such skill, is unmistakably foreshadowed. It would appear that Hepplewhite was testing how far he could indulge his own leanings without breaking away altogether from the established mode, just as he occasionally applied Chinese fretwork to his bookshelves and china-brackets.

Through much of his work there is an undercurrent of French tradition, and he gives us the special make of sofa which Adam patronised, with the name of "Confidante" to confess its foreign origin. No elegant drawing-room, he tells us, could be considered complete without one. Nor were they, if we may judge from the frequently recurring "confidante in barre damask" in the sale lists of a century ago. This article of furniture was an ordinary stuffed couch with seats at the ends all made in one, to enable a few friends to converse. It was sometimes constructed

FIG. 141.—CONFIDANTE. Hepplewhite.

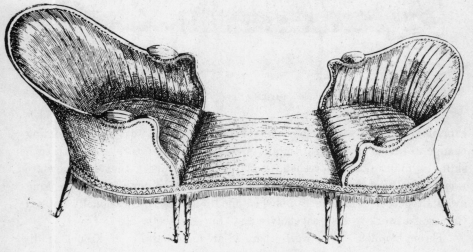

FIG. 142.—DUCHESSE. Hepplewhite.

so that the ends could be taken away and used separately as two Burjair chairs. "Duchesse," as its name implies, was another Parisian adaptation, and consisted of two Burjair chairs put together with a stool in

FIG. 143.—HEPPLEWHITE SIDEBOARD.

the centre, greatly resembling the French bed, from which the idea was derived; indeed a tester and covering were sometimes added. Neither of these designs had any lasting popularity in England, certainly not nearly as much as was awarded to his bar-backed sofa, which, notwithstanding its "busy" lines, is still much sought after as an example of his work.

Hepplewhite's little "window stools" shown in our larger group are among his best designs, and though the classic feeling is as clearly emphasised as in Adam's, the idea originally came from France. Their dimensions were intended to be governed by the space they were to fill, the height of the seat being that of an ordinary chair. They were manufactured in satin-wood, with painted or japanned ornament, and the seats covered with "taberray or morine of a pea-green or other light colour." The severe simplicity of their lines, combined with the general grace, would seem to have made them eminently fitted to hold their own in the coming change of taste brought about by Sheraton, yet their reign only lasted to the end of the century. Besides these, Hepplewhite improved the ordinary stool, which he designed in various graceful forms for music or dressing rooms.

Hepplewhite's sideboards were interesting not only artistically but historically. The two designs he gives have deep cellarettes at the ends with drawers above, and another, long and shallow, in the centre. They are very similar to one of Shearer's designs, and suggest that this style of sideboard was not the idea of any one man in particular, but of the cabinet-makers of the time. The sideboard, under Chippendale's hands, had been more or less a continuation of the slab table, with very little structural change. In fact, by omitting drawers, he took the article back instead of forward; for even in 1746, as Mr. Lyon points out in his *Colonial Furniture*, sideboards with "lavatories" and "bottle cisterns" existed. Adam's design varied little from Chippendale's in outward form, except in the occasional addition of pedestals. Hepplewhite and Shearer were more revolutionary. They greatly improved it in appearance by introducing flowing curves, while also attending to its usefulness as a storage place for the indispensable adjuncts of the dining-room. The space allotted for the latter purpose was limited in size, though it included not only room for wine and plate, but a drawer in which water might be kept for washing glasses. It has been suggested that the curved and *bombé* fronts which distinguish Hepplewhite's furniture would seem to have been a recognition in wood of Hogarth's " Line of Beauty," and this is probably so.   In any case, it is certain that wherever Hepplewhite could resort to curvilinear form he did so, sometimes overreaching his aim, but more often gaining elegance, especially in the fronts of his larger pieces.

The loose pedestal illustrated served as an adjunct to the " sideboard table " or cupboard sideboard " in spacious dining - rooms," and was surmounted by graceful wood or metal urns for holding iced water.

FIG. 144.—SIDEBOARD WITHOUT DRAWERS, AND HEPPLEWHITE TRAY AND TEA-CADDIES.

The brass-hooped cellarettes which Hepplewhite called " gardes du vin " were devised to fill up the space under the open sideboard, to use when there were no drawers ; and from their early tub-like shape developed into classic and refined pieces of carved work, till at length they died after degenerating into the hideous sarcophagi which Sheraton tells us were " generally adopted in their place by the higher classes " about the beginning of the present century.

It is impossible now to say with any certainty to whom the praise justly belongs for the improvement effected in sideboards.   But, reasoning on what we know of the other work of the two men, it is likely that it was a composite production; Shearer evolving the useful, and Hepplewhite the ornamental. In any case, they paved the way for Sheraton, who developed their designs in both particulars, and produced a piece of furniture which not only possessed all the beauty required by the eye of an artist, but all the usefulness that could gladden that of the careful housewife.

In Hepplewhite's designs we see many improvements on articles which

FIG. 145.—PEDESTAL AND VASE. Hepplewhite.   FIG. 146.—CELLARETTE. Hepplewhite.

had been for long in common use in England, such as bureaux, desks, and chests of drawers. He saw that these were, and always would be, required in some form or other to suit English habits; so, while bringing them to what he considered elegant requirements, he left their utilitarian qualities undisturbed. Furniture for writing purposes had been in use for centuries, under the names of "desks," "scrutoirs," or "bureaux," and their various forms were in common use. Probably about the beginning of the eighteenth century bookcases or cabinet tops began to be added to them. Chippendale and his followers published designs for these, both with and without cabriole legs, under the name of "desks and bookcases."

Bureaux pure and simple were evidently even then being relegated to common rooms in the houses of the higher class, and writing-tables and French adaptations were taking their place.   Hepplewhite as well as Sheraton

FIG. 147.—DESK AND BOOKCASE.   Hepplewhite.

must be credited with making this form again popular by the lightness of style, all the decorations added being of the most refined kind.   Though careful, and, to a certain extent, successful in the general contour of his pieces, it is not to his eye for form in masses that Hepplewhite owes his name, but to the exquisitely designed and artistically executed inlay with

which he decorated his furniture. To add to the general feeling of rich-
ness and elegance, he even went so far as to construct the inside of the
bureaux and writing-tables entirely of satin-wood. The skill which he
displayed in producing the geometrical mouldings of the glass panel in
the cabinet doors, as well as his mastery of curve, is shown in Fig. 147.

FIG. 148.—TAMBOUR WRITING-TABLE.   Hepplewhite.

These scroll panels were often radiating ovals or even still more clever and
complicated, as he and the other designers invested them with the same
lines their cabinets possessed, inlaid them, if the decoration was inlay, or
carved them, if that supplied the *motif* of the whole, besides frequently
making them of brass or other metal painted to suit the woodwork.

Hepplewhite also published designs for secretaries and bookcases,
differing, he says, from the desk and bookcase "in not being sloped
in front. The accommodations, therefore, are produced by the face of

the upper drawer falling down by means of a spring and quadrant, which produces the same usefulness as the front of a desk." Secretaries

FIG. 149.—TAMBOUR WRITING-TABLE AND BOOKCASE.   Hepplewhite.

with sliding covers for the desk (the "bureau à cylindre," which sprang up in France about 1750) are called by Hepplewhite "Tambour writing-tables," and "answer all the purposes of a desk, with a lighter appearance."

The "reeded" top, with its alternate lines of satin-wood and mahogany, was a favourite with this maker; for he uses it with a bookcase top over, and though the effect as a whole is not homogeneous, we can almost forget the weakness of the design in admiring the lovely "metal frames" in the bookcase doors.   His strong point lay, not always in the design itself, but in its enrichment.   His commodes, card, pier, and Pembroke tables, for instance, attain beauty from the inlay of various coloured woods and the skilful way in which they were painted.   Sometimes the inlay and painting are so wonderfully blended that it is difficult to tell, without close examination, where one begins and the other ends, the shaded parts on the light woods being as often got by one means as the other. Much of the success of this treatment must be due to the loving skill of the artists who lent him their aid, but the construction and inlay are purely the work of the Hepplewhite firm.

In Hepplewhite's time, tea had come to be more generally used by the nation, though costing almost a sovereign a pound, and, true to his desire to provide articles required by English customs and habits, he made all articles connected with it his peculiar care.   Quaint little urn-stands for the breakfast-table, with small slides at the side to rest the teapot on, elaborate tea-trays inlaid with coloured woods, tea-chests and tea-caddies of delicate marquetry, are among his choicest wares.

Hepplewhite bestowed much attention on bedroom furniture.   His beds are simpler than those of most of the other designers of his time, but his bedposts, which he mainly carved with leaves and wheat-ears, do not approach the beauty of Chippendale's.   It is curious that, in spite of his close connection with Shearer, he was much less affected by his mechanical inventions than one would have expected, while Sheraton, in some of his phases, might easily be mistaken for Shearer.   Hepplewhite gives no surprising harlequin machinery in the opening lids of his dressing-tables, which either open at the back or sides, and the compartments contained in them and his "dressing drawers" are of the ordinary kind. These were often made in satin-wood altogether, for so many rare woods had been imported by this time that Hepplewhite sometimes rather slightingly gives permission for these tables to be "made of mahogany or other inferior wood."   The external shape of some of the folding tables is the same as Shearer's, with the addition of fluting to the legs, but it would have been very difficult to add anything in the way of improvement to the comprehensive arrangements the Cabinet-makers' Society had already planned.

The one great mechanical contrivance is Rudd's reflecting dressing-

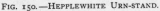

FIG. 150.—HEPPLEWHITE URN-STAND.   FIG. 151.—HEPPLEWHITE BED-POST.

table, "possessing every convenience which can be wanted, or mechanism and ingenuity supply." "The middle drawer slides by itself. The two end drawers are framed to the sides A, and fasten at the catch B; and when disengaged, each drawer swings horizontally on a centre pin at C, and may be placed in any station as shown in the drawing. The glasses turn upward, and are supported by a spring at the bottom of the quadrant, which pushed in, they fall down and slide under with the two end drawers. They also swing on pins DD. E is a slide covered with green cloth for writing on; F the bolt of the lock, which shoots into the lower rail." The name of this wonderful table, he tells us, is reported to have been derived from that of a once popular character for whom it was first made, and the illustration will give some idea of its wonders. Sheraton, in his

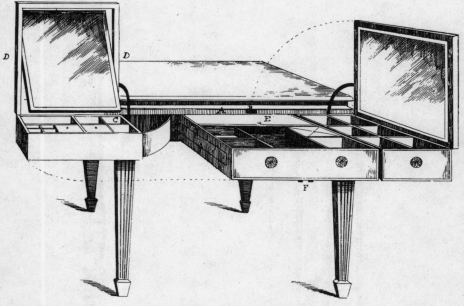

FIG. 152.—RUDD'S REFLECTING DRESSING-TABLE. Hepplewhite.

Dictionary, rather sarcastically observes that the advantage of being able to see the back part of the head as well as the front is a mere trifle compared with the expense it occasions.

After this outburst of ingenuity, supposing that the invention was really his own, (which is doubtful as Shearer's Lady's Dressing Table is exactly the same,) he returns to ordinary square shaving-tables resembling Chippendale's plainer kinds, but with inlay instead of carving. Among other articles for bedroom use are corner basin-stands, which were very common about this time, as they were "a useful shape, and standing in a

corner were out of the way." The "clothes press" of the Chippendale
era had also advanced a stage towards modern times and become a "wardrobe" by name without much change in its accommodation, for it was still
only supplied with sliding shelves. Sheraton was the first to introduce
wardrobes in which clothes might be hung, for hitherto the large cupboards,
almost rooms in themselves, built into every old house, rendered such

FIG. 153.—CORNER WASHSTAND. Hepplewhite.

pieces of bedroom furniture unnecessary. Toilet glasses were greatly
improved by the oval form Hepplewhite employed, as well as by his more
distinctive heart-shape, the serpentine-fronted stands of which were
enriched with shell and fan marquetry.

Chests of drawers had been made in this country for over a hundred
years, and were such "articles of general use and service" in England
that they naturally ensured Hepplewhite's attention. Principally made
of oak before the Chippendale era, the small sizes were often used for
dressing-tables as well; but when separate pieces of furniture were made

for toilet purposes, the chests of drawers grew higher and higher. Their flat tops were sometimes finished with an arched pediment, or with special contrivances called steps for the display of china. Chippendale favoured these "tall-boys" or "high-boys," as they were called, in his appointments for bedrooms, and made his "buroe" or common dressing-tables also answer the purpose of the small chest of drawers. Hepplewhite did

FIG. 154.—HEPPLEWHITE DRESSING-GLASS.

not attempt to supersede the old shapes, but merely took them in hand and added his peculiar style of decoration and any improvements he could devise. His smaller sets have his favourite serpentine fronts and sides, with beautifully inlaid or painted decoration. The dressing chests of drawers are the same shape outwardly, but the inside of the upper drawer is covered by a cloth slide and contains mirrors and "necessary dressing equipage" so as to dispense with a separate toilet-table. His double sets reach to the floor, and have flat or urn-crowned tops. The slide between the two divisions is usually supposed to have been intended for writing, but it is much more probable that it was used to place the clothes upon while they were being brushed and folded.

Most of Hepplewhite's hanging lamps, mirrors, girandoles, pier-glasses, and cornices reflect Adam's ideas, with an added freedom of ornament

FIG. 155.—DOUBLE CHEST OF DRAWERS.   Hepplewhite.

which gives greater grace of style ; but he confined himself almost entirely within his province of cabinet-making, and did not attempt grates, metal-work, or architectural fittings.   The Hepplewhites had not been educated in the same rigid school as the Adams, and the flowing Italian lines of Pergolesi and Columbani appealed to them more than the extreme formality of the strictly classic school.   Their brackets of burnished gold for supporting clocks, busts, and lamps, like those made for the " large subscription room at Newmarket," have more flowing beauty but less architectural value than we find in Adam; while their candle-stands are quite unlike any by the other designers, and, with the graceful branches of lacquered brass, must have been ornamental as well as " very useful in drawing-rooms, halls, and large staircases."

The Hepplewhite commode has long been obsolete or transformed into

FIG. 156.—GIRANDOLE.   Hepplewhite.

the modern cabinet with mirror back, but in the Georgian era no drawing-room with any pretensions to fashion was complete without one. The square or oval shape which Adam originated and brought into vogue differed entirely from the very French commode of Chippendale and the Louis Quinze period. It was always placed below the tall mirror in the spacious reception rooms, and the size adapted to the space it was required to fill. Hepplewhite and Shearer adopted the circular form and endowed it with the same sobriety of English taste and style which they helped to

FIG. 157.—BRACKET.   Hepplewhite.

FIG. 158.—BRACKET.   Hepplewhite.

spread throughout the country.   It gave them an excellent opportunity for

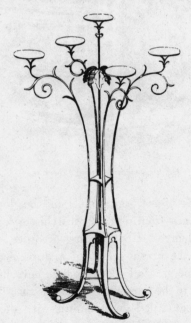

FIG. 159.—CANDLE-STAND.   Hepplewhite.

uniting the "elegance and utility" upon which they prided themselves.
Being "intended for use in the principal rooms," it required "considerable
elegance" externally, while "the shelves within answered the purpose of
a closet or cupboard." "The panels may be of satin-wood" painted or
inlaid, "and the top, and also the borders and front, are frequently
enriched with painted or inlaid work." The decoration of these commodes

FIG. 160.—HEPPLEWHITE COMMODE.

was often quite a work of art, the panels in the doors having ovals of
dancing nymphs or scenes from mythological history painted by the early
members of the Academy. Hepplewhite accorded them the place of
honour in his plan of the arrangement of a drawing-room "which, being
a state room, should possess all the elegance embellishments can give."
The chimney-piece was to be flanked by sofas, with a "confidante" on the
opposite side. Small seats filled the windows, with pier-tables surmounted
by square glasses between, while an "elegant commode" and chairs filled

the space from door to door. Sheraton adhered to the same disposition of furniture, and most drawing-rooms of the day were in similar fashion. "For a dining-room, instead of the pier, there should be a set of dining tables," and a sideboard substituted for a commode. "The rest of the furniture, and general ordonnance of the room is equally proper, except the square glass over the sofa, which might be omitted ; but this is mere opinion, many of the dining-parlours of our first nobility having full as much glass as is here shown." Hepplewhite, having thus provided for the principal rooms of an ordinary house, brings his list of modest and useful designs to a

FIG. 161.—LADY'S WORK-TABLE.   Hepplewhite.

close. The more they are studied the more it becomes apparent that it is to them, rather than to those by Chippendale, that we owe the revival of eighteenth-century designs in present-day furniture. Almost all the illustrations could be copied and used, while their form is already taken as the basis of a great deal of modern furnishing.

When the over-strained fancies of the preceding school are recalled, Hepplewhite's more simple lines, but delicately playful inlay, are almost a relief, notwithstanding the disposition to flimsiness in some of his carved ornament. There is the same culture and restraint which the Adams exhibited, but the greater liberality of his views is expressed by the large number and varying designs for the table, tray, and commode tops. Possessing all the advantages of a transition period, his furniture retains some of the sweeping lines of the past, and yet is happily influenced by the refined classicism which became intensified in his successors. The Hepplewhite firm advanced English cabinet-making in the direction of greater sobriety of taste without any serious loss of the beauty which had already been developed. It is customary to class all this style and period as " Adams " ; but, though the classical form was entirely introduced by them both in their work and furnishings, it would never have attained any widespread popularity had it not been continued and amplified by these cabinet-makers. Adam's furniture is only adapted to houses on the same lines, while that of Hepplewhite is equally applicable to a less restricted style of architecture.

Looking at Hepplewhite's work as a whole, one can barely fail to be struck by its inequality. He might be called the Romney of cabinet-makers, at times rising to positive genius, and challenging comparison with the best work of any era, then again producing mere common-places which, without his name attached to them, would be passed over without even transitory notice. He certainly did not possess either the innate feeling of Chippendale or the knowledge of Sheraton. His work gives the impression of being designed on the spur of the moment ; and though this led, in many instances, to something approaching inspiration, it is impossible altogether to forget the times when the transient whim of his brain was mistaken for the divine afflatus. Chippendale was so absolute that he was generally right even when most wrong; Sheraton, immersed in theory, was often least interesting when most right by his rules. Each of these men came more or less up to their own standards ; but when Hepplewhite sat down to make a design, it would seem to have been a mere matter of chance whether he produced a work of art which should go down to all time, or something which his admirers would most willingly forget.

VIII

THOMAS SHERATON

THOMAS SHERATON, last of the furniture designers of the eighteenth century, was second only to Chippendale in power and appreciation of beauty. He probably began his career when Chippendale's fame was at its zenith, and he must have lived to see the beginning of the wave of bad taste that swept all beauty from English furniture. When we now look back on the long list of designers and architects of the last century, one succeeding another without a gap, the fact that Sheraton was the last, and that after him came the deluge, seems capable of no explanation whatever. The dying out of the "man of taste," who had done the grand tour, and who looked on a trained critical faculty as one of the first essentials of the gentleman, may have been partly accountable. To this must be added the fostering of our insular prejudices by the period of our history which saw England stand practically alone against the whole of Europe. And even now, though a century has gone by since the publication of Sheraton's book, and another art wave has arisen, our furniture has not attained the excellence of the bygone time. Our schools of design (so called) seem to have done us little good. They are simply hotbeds for forcing into life the incompetent painter. The master craftsman is dead, and there is no immediate likelihood of his being resuscitated. It is all but a positive certainty that, had Chippendale and Sheraton lived in our time, instead of being, as they now are, undying names, they would, if remembered by posterity at all, only be so remembered as painters of mediocre pictures. But the atmosphere of the eighteenth century was more favourable to the growth of art in this direction. Our ancestors insisted on getting a first-rate article, and had not our objections to paying for it. The craftsman was a man of substance and education, and though he was a little too ready to take

FIG. 162.—A SHERATON ROOM.

his hat in his hand and sue for the patronage of some little-great man, there was nothing of the snob about him. He designed his own goods, helped with his own hands in their construction, and sold them himself in his own shop. From start to finish, the impress of his mind and hand was on every article. He was not selling goods sweated in Whitechapel, and hurriedly run together out of any timber that could be procured at a cheap enough figure. From the careful choosing of the wood to the final touches on the article manufactured, everything had either been done by himself or under his own eye, and each object he sold was an old friend in which he took both pride and pleasure. Pedantic he certainly was, and Thomas Sheraton possibly the most pedantic of all, judging from his publication, *The Cabinet-maker and Upholsterer's Drawing-book*, 1791 (with an Appendix, 1793, and an Accompaniment, 1794). Chippendale's five orders are nothing to what Sheraton thinks necessary to prove his capacity. Two hundred and fifty-four pages are allotted to perspective, but this part of the book is utterly valueless. That Sheraton understood perspective himself in a theoretical way is amply shown, but if he learnt it from a master who had no greater gift of making the principles clear than he had himself, he was worthy of the very highest admiration.

He expresses surprise at the total absence of the necessary instruction for drawing furniture, and, reviewing the number of books that had been published between the date of his own work and Chippendale's, says, " Books of various designs in cabinet work, ornamented according to the taste of the times in which they were published, have already appeared. But none of these, as far as I know, profess to give any instructions relative to the art of making perspective drawings, or to treat of such geometrical lines as ought to be known by persons of both professions, especially such of them as have a number of men under their direction."

He does not speak very respectfully of his brother designers, but goes on to say: " As I have alluded to some books of designs, it may be proper here just to say something of them. I have seen one which seems to have been published before Chippendale's. I infer this from the antique appearance of the furniture, for there is no date to it; but the title informs us that it was composed by a Society of Cabinet-makers in London. It gives no instructions for drawing in any form, but we may venture to say that those who drew the designs wanted a good share of teaching themselves.

"Chippendale's book seems to be next in order to this, but the former is without comparison to it, either as to size or real merit. Chippendale's book has, it is true, given us the proportions of the five orders, and lines for two or three cases, which is all it pretends to relative to rules for drawing; and, as for the designs themselves, they are now wholly antiquated and laid aside, though possessed of great merit, according to the times in which they were executed."

Speaking of Manwaring's book, he says: "This publication professes to show the method of striking out all kinds of bevel work, by which, as the author says, the most ignorant person will be immediately acquainted with what many artists have served seven years to know. But this assertion both exceeds the bounds of modesty and truth, since there is nothing in his directions for bevel work, which he parades so much about, but what an apprentice boy may be taught by seven hours' proper instructions." Of his chairs he remarks that "they are nearly as old as Chippendale's, and seem to be copied from them." He considers Ince and Mayhew's book "to have been a book of merit in its day, though much inferior to Chippendale's, which was a real original, as well as more extensive and masterly in its designs."

Again, as to Hepplewhite. "Some of these designs are not without merit, though it is evident that the perspective is, in some instances, erroneous. But, notwithstanding the late date of Heppelwhite's book, if we compare some of the designs, particularly the chairs, with the newest taste, we shall find that this work has already caught the decline, and perhaps, in a little time will suddenly die in the disorder. This instance may serve to convince us of that fate which all books of the same kind will ever be subject to. . . . I shall now conclude this account of books of designs with observing, that in the same year was given a quarto book of different pieces of furniture, with the *Cabinet-makers' London Book of Prices;* and, considering that it did not make its appearance under the title of a book of designs, but only to illustrate the prices, it certainly lays claim to merit, and does honour to the publishers. Upon the whole then, if the intended publication, which now petitions your patronage and support, be so compiled and composed as fully to answer, and also to merit, the title which has been given to it, I think it will be found greatly to supply the defects of those books now mentioned, and will appear to be on as lasting a foundation as can well be expected in a work of this kind." The book, or what we may consider the book, begins on page 289, and is really a most important, if not *the* most important addition to the subject. His directions are minute in the extreme, and prove him to have been a thorough workman, to whom no point was so small as not to require care and judgment.

A few scattered quotations from his lengthy instructions on the

FIG. 163.—SHERATON SOFA.

making of a " universal table" may be of interest. It is quite a plain piece of furniture of the *multum in parvo* description, but there are three full pages of instructions. "The framing is three inches broad, and mitred at the corners; and the panels are sometimes glued up in three thicknesses, the middle piece being laid with the grain across, and the other two lengthways of the panel, to prevent its warping. . . . When the panels are tongued into the framing, and the mitres are fitted to, the tops should stand to shrink as much as possible before they are glued for good. There are different methods of securing the mitres of the framing. Some make simply a straight mitre, . . . but the strongest method is to mortice and tenon the mitres together, having a square joint at the under, and a mitre joint at the upper side. . . . In gluing the mitres, it will be proper, first, to glue on the outside of each mitre a piece of deal in the shape of a wedge, which will take a hand-screw, so that when they are putting together, the glue may be brought out, and the mitres made close. . . . To save expense, the tops have been found to answer the purpose in solid wood, without being framed. When they are made in this manner, particular regard should be had

FIG. 164.—MAHOGANY AND BRASS CHAIR.
In the South Kensington Museum. Sheraton.

FIG. 165.—INLAID SATIN-WOOD CHAIR.
In the South Kensington Museum. Sheraton.

to placing the heart side of the wood outward, which naturally draws round of itself, and may therefore be expected to keep true, notwith-standing its unfavourable situation."

When we read page after page of minute instructions like these, we begin to understand how it is that the furniture made by Sheraton, with all its seeming fragility, and sometimes a leaning to unsound constructive principles, has stood the test of time in the wonderful way it has. The sofa we illustrate (Fig. 163) is in actual and constant use, and, in spite of the flimsy manner in which the back and arms are joined on to the uprights, is still in perfect repair, and likely to remain so for an indefinite period. It is made of satin-wood with mahogany inlay, and the carving is a fine example of Sheraton's work. The piece is instructive as showing his use of French designs. His model for this particular sofa was evidently French of the late period of Louis Seize, and his alteration of the original is characteristic. The general lines are kept, but the redundancy of ornament is eschewed. He replaces the too floreate carving by plain

FIG. 166.—DRAWING-ROOM CHAIR.   Taken from the French.   Sheraton.

inlay, and what carving he gives does not in the least interfere with his severer line.

The two drawings of chairs from the South Kensington Museum are very fine examples of workmanship, as well as of Sheraton's different styles. They are simple and graceful in design, and the inlay and carving show him at his best. The lyre in furniture was almost unknown in England till the end of last century, and Sheraton must have the credit of applying the idea generally, though Adam had previously suggested it. The strings at the back and sides, as well as some of the ornamental bosses, are brass, the metal contrasting well with the dark mahogany. The high-backed chair is of satin-wood, with rosewood inlay, and the engraved panels were probably produced by the application of a red-hot needle. Though the label describes it as only "probably by Sheraton," it bears such a strong resemblance to his designs that we may consider it to be authentic. These chairs are very pretty to look at, but as regards construction and comfort they fail. The back of this chair, which is particularly high, thus increasing the leverage, has a splat which is some distance above the body of the chair; while in the arm-chair, where the leverage is of little or no consequence because of the support given by the arms, the splat runs into the back of the seat. With a low seat one naturally does not keep one's body so straight as in a high one, so Sheraton attends to our deportment, instead of our ease, by providing a high support which makes leaning back an impossibility; while in the arm-chair he departs from his customary severity of line to provide an ornamental knob on the top rail, rather painfully reminiscent of the Inquisition. Our grandfathers must have been a straight-backed, hardy race, if they found rest and comfort in chairs like these after a hard day's work.

These objections cannot be urged against the stuffed-back "drawing-room chair," which certainly lacks nothing in the way of comfort. It is wanting in originality, however, being merely an adaptation of the French of Louis Seize. Indeed, just as Chippendale followed the earlier period, so did Sheraton copy the later furnishings. The pendulum of fashion in France had swung from the over-ornamentation of the rococo to the purer outlines of classic renaissance, and architecture had led the way in this as it had done previously. The rebuilding of Versailles by Gabriel in severer form turned the public taste, just as in our own country the architectural work of Adam began the Græco-Roman revival. Sheraton was quick to perceive the beauties and adaptabilities of this style, and largely used classic ornament and detail, reproducing it in the form of marquetry, with carving added only as an accessory. Like Chippendale, he borrowed the idea, but translated it in a different form. Sometimes he made only a slavish copy to begin with, as in the case of this drawing-room chair, which is thoroughly Louis Seize in feeling, while the other on the same page of his book (reproduced in our large group) is his own variation on the theme. The copy is not confined to the outline of the square back and turned legs, but even extends to the gilding and coverings. Sheraton thus describes the way he wishes this carried out: "The frame is intended to be finished in burnished gold, and the seat and back covered with printed silk. In the front rail is a tablet, with a little carving in its panel. The legs and stumps have twisted flutes and fillets, done in the turning, which produce a good effect in the gold."

The other chair has more of the Sheraton touch, especially in the back, and he recommends it to be finished in japan painting, with a little gilding interspersed in different parts of the banister, while the seat is to be of the less expensive material beginning to be made for this purpose in England, "printed chintz with border to suit." The fashion for coloured decoration

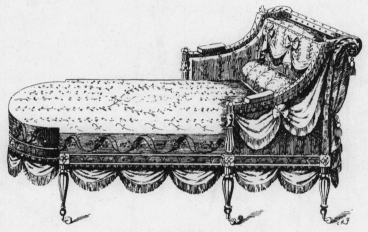

FIG. 167.—CHAISE LONGUE. Sheraton.

had led to all sorts of French silks and satins being used on the chair seats in place of the plainer morocco and horsehair, and Sheraton even advises a poor imitation of cut-out and pasted-on work which took for a time. "Chairs of this kind have an effect which far exceeds any conception we can have of them from an uncoloured engraving, or even of a coloured one."

Notwithstanding the constant wars with France, and the deep hatred occasioned by the dread of Napoleon's continual aggressions, French fashions in furniture were even more studied by Sheraton than by any of his predecessors. The older he grew, the more French his work became, till at last almost all trace of an English foundation disappeared, and he sank into little more than a slavish copyist of things Parisian. His punishment was severe enough, for even in 1802 we find him lamenting "that a clumsy four-footed stool from France will be admired by our connoisseurs, in preference to a first-rate cabinet of English production." He holds that we have brought this upon ourselves by "foolishly staring after French fashions, instead of exerting ourselves to improve our own, by granting suitable encouragement to designers and artists for that

FIG. 168.—DRAWING-ROOM CHAIR WITH TRACES OF CHIPPENDALE.   Sheraton.

purpose. Instead of this, when our tradesmen are desirous to draw the best customers to their warerooms, they hasten over to Paris, or otherwise pretend to go there, plainly indicating either our own defects in cabinet-making, or extreme ignorance, that we must be pleased and attracted by the mere sound of French taste." Too late he poses as the champion of English trade by proposing the establishment of public brass-foundries and wood-yards, and the employment of "a superintender to give directions to the manufacturer," in imitation of the French Government.

Sheraton eschewed the cabriole leg of Chippendale, and though often using a tapering square, seems to have preferred turnery. He originated the most intricate ornament both for the legs and backs of his chairs, and gives pages of designs for square and banister shapes, in some of which traces of Chippendale appear. Only in two cases is Hepplewhite's shield form resorted to, for Sheraton evidently considered this antiquated. Some of the

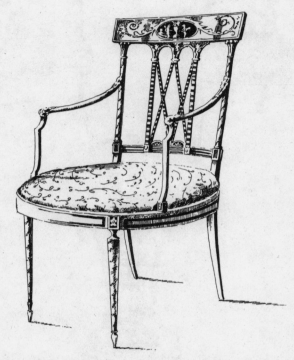

FIG. 169.—SHERATON DRAWING-ROOM CHAIR WITH FLAT BACK REST.

chairs have flat tops derived from old Greek models, and these are slightly hollowed to serve as a rest to the back. He kept to this form very much in his later work, and most drawing-room chairs in the early years of the present century were modelled upon it. It was comfortable, almost as comfortable as his ingenious idea for a conversation chair, which is here given in his own "sudden" perspective, thereby saving the time and trouble of representing the back legs. Unfortunately it can only be used by the male sex, as the proper position for the sitter is facing the back of the chair, with the arms resting on the top rail, and was doubtless devised for the

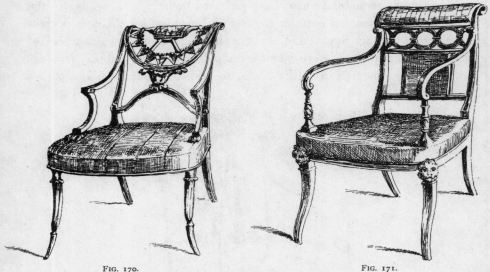

FIG. 170.

FIG. 171.

DRAWING-ROOM CHAIRS IN SHERATON'S LATER STYLE (1802).

FIG. 172.—SHERATON'S CONVERSATION CHAIR.

benefit of the beaux of the Georgian time, whose coat tails were far too costly
to be sat upon.

The vertical lines of this old master's chairs are almost invariably straight, with a well-shaped vase or lyre ornament forming the back ; and one of his favourite ways of varying the form of the top rail was to place a painted or inlaid panel directly over the splat. The legs, if square, had a carving of husks carried down the front. The acanthus was generally

FIG. 173.—SHERATON CHAIR WITH VASE ORNAMENT IN THE BACK.

used for the scroll carving, while the paterae were formed of laurel leaves. Like Hepplewhite, traces of his connection with the Prince of Wales survive in the carved or painted plume of feathers. The splats and banisters of his chairs were sometimes inlaid with lighter woods, and the dark mahogany dining-room chairs relieved with brass. But he, or the public, tired of carved and inlaid woods, and so he " racked his invention " for a new idea, and resorted to gilded and painted furniture. Here the classic severity lay merely in the outline, for the decoration itself rivals the productions of the most ornate French school. Carved satin-wood picked out with gilding, cameo panels in grisaille, or the most gorgeously coloured wreaths, flowers, cornucopia, and musical instruments were painted on the chairs and cabinets. In fact, whatever would add to the beauty and enrichment

FIG. 174.—PAINTED DRAWING-ROOM CHAIR.   Sheraton.

was pressed into service, and large sums were frequently spent on a single chair back. Sheraton continually suggests that "the ornament may be white and gold, japanned or painted," while he reminds us that a drawing-room admits of the highest taste and elegance. The Gothic and Chinese designs with which Chippendale decorated his walls and ceilings were quite discarded, and the classic style generally employed. Sheraton used panels and groups, surrounded with flowers and foliage, such as were common in the boudoirs of Marie Antoinette and the French Court at that time.   Even mantelpieces were constructed of satin-wood or mahogany, and painted to match.   The plan and sections of the drawing-room given in his book show figure panels on the walls, pier-tables, square mirrors, and carefully arranged draperies, more straight and stiff than those of Hepplewhite, and with even more expensive decoration ; for the windows have Corinthian

Fig. 175.—Painted Drawing-room Chair.   Sheraton.

pilasters, and " the cove and ceilings are to be richly ornamented in paintings and gold."   In describing the commode intended to occupy the central piece in one of the walls, he says : " In the frieze part is a tablet in the centre made of an exquisite composition in imitation of statuary marble.   These are to be had, of any figure or any subject, at Mr. Wedgwood's in Soho Square."   "The commode should be painted to suit the furniture, and the legs and other parts in gold to harmonise with the sofas, tables, and chairs."   We must remember that Sheraton designed rooms and furniture for the Prince of Wales (afterwards George the Fourth) and most of the nobility, so he was not hampered by any economical considerations. He went so far in the service of royalty as to forget his principles and to ornament a room in the old form of Chinese for the " first gentleman in Europe "; but he must have had some misgivings deep down in his heart, for he says, " The effect of the whole, though it may appear extravagant to a vulgar eye, is most suitable to the dignity of the proprietor."

FIG. 176.—TRIPOD. FIRE-SCREEN.

If this old cabinet-maker sometimes forgot his highest aims, or lost sight of the practical use of his chairs in their elaborate decorations, still his fine thought in planning other articles deserves only the most unstinted praise. From his " summer bed," in which he leaves a passage between the two compartments " for the circulation of air," and likewise " to afford an easy access to the servants when they make the beds," and the sideboard with a hollow front, specially made for the butler to reach across it, and also to secure him from the " jostles of the other servants if the sideboard is placed near the door," down to the many ingeniously contrived articles of combined use, he seems to have considered almost everything. Sheraton confesses to admiring Shearer's work, and there are strong points of resemblance between

many of their articles.   Sheraton's cylinder desk and bookcase is like
Shearer's writing and toilet tables in the lower part, though the tops differ.
Both cabinet-makers give the same little corner wash-stands, and the dress-

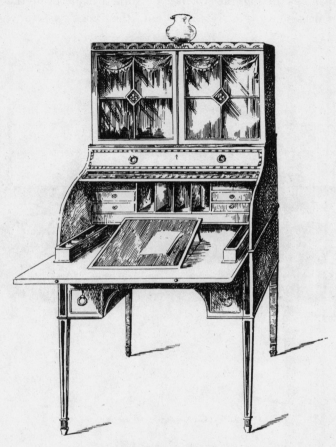

Fig. 177.—Cylinder Desk and Bookcase.   Sheraton.

ing and toilet arrangements are almost identical.   The "Harlequin" table
is one of the numerous ingenious pieces of mechanism we are continually
finding in both designers.   In many of these latter Sheraton out-Shearered
Shearer, not only in the cleverness of his inventions, but, as we would expect
from his powers, in artistic merit as well.

There is not much difference between Hepplewhite's and Sheraton's

treatment of dining - room furniture. The sideboard designed by the
latter follows closely on the same lines as that designed by the former,
though with a more rigid adherence to the classic, and the addition of
several ingenious fittings all Sheraton's own. Sometimes the pedestals
of his predecessors were retained, but the front was brought more

FIG. 178.—SHERATON SIDEBOARD.

forward and supported on carved and tapering legs. All sorts of conveniences for the butler's use were enclosed in the drawers or pedestals.
One division contained the cellarette made to draw out separately from
the rest, and sometimes large enough to contain ten or twelve wine-
bottles. The back part of the other side was lined with green baize,
while the front was fitted up as a sink for washing knives and spoons,
which, then more limited in number than they are now, were washed in the
room and used again immediately. In some sideboards there was a rack

to stand the plates in, and the cupboard was lined all round with lead to
retain the warmth from the heater placed below.   Many other ingenious
contrivances were planned by Sheraton: shelves for glasses, or a sliding
tambour door in front, and perhaps a wooden moulding along the top to
prevent the plates or silver slipping forward.   The vase knife-boxes were

FIG. 179.—SIDEBOARD WITH VASE KNIFE-CASES.   Sheraton.

sometimes made of japanned copper, but oftener of inlaid mahogany and
satin-wood.   They had by this time become so elaborate that they formed
a special manufacture, for their curves required so much knowledge
and skill that only the best cabinet-makers were allowed to adopt this
branch of work.   The ornamental brass-work at the back marked an
advance on the previous simple rail, and supported candle-branches,
"which, when lighted, give a very brilliant effect to the silver ware."
A convex glass was occasionally hung within the centre circle, and was

united with the rail in Sheraton's later designs, affording the idea for the afterwards more enlarged mirror back.

Sheraton and Hepplewhite tried to keep up the dresser form, and succeeded for a time. The former says, "There are other sideboards for small dining-rooms made without drawers or pedestals, but have generally a wine-cooler to stand under them, hooped with brass, partitioned and lined with lead for wine-bottles, the same as the before-mentioned cellarette drawers"; and in his *Dictionary* in 1803 he tells us, "The most fashionable sideboards at present are those without cellarettes, or any kind of drawer, having massy ornamented legs, and moulded frames."

Sheraton extended the use of mahogany by his selection of beautifully marked varieties for his veneers, and these he inlaid with bandings of satin

FIG. 180.—SARCOPHAGUS WINE CISTERN. Sheraton (1803).

and other woods, his feeling for colour leading him to prefer inlay to carving for his decorations. Occasionally the cabinets, chairs, or tables were made entirely of the finest satin-wood, far more beautiful than our modern specimens; for, like the early mahogany, it was of beautiful colouring and rich figure in the grain. These were frequently inlaid with natural coloured or artificially stained woods, and had marquetry or painted ovals in addition.

Sheraton's work is generally noted for its curved surfaces, the graceful sweeps of his sideboards and cabinets reflecting the light and forming a pleasing contrast to the straightness of the vertical lines. Simplicity of outline is one of his greatest characteristics, and, even in the more elaborate designs, he seldom, if ever, allows his decoration to interfere with the character of his work as a whole. That he was sometimes given to preposterous ornament his designs for state beds prove, but, as a rule, he is much more practical and severe than any of the designers who went before him.

Drawing-room cabinets made a great advance in Sheraton's time. His predecessors had plenty of console-tables with mirrors over, and even some sort of a cabinet or "china-case," but Sheraton undoubtedly first introduced the kind which has been, with many variations, in use for the last hundred years. The design sketched in Fig. 181 has been the model for many hundreds since. Though the *motif* may be perhaps originally traced to the

FIG. 181.—DRAWING-ROOM CABINET. Sheraton.

Court of Louis XVI., yet it would be difficult to find any special design of which it is a reproduction. It is purely Sheraton,—Sheraton at his best,— and fully illustrates the combined simplicity and utility of his style. The grace of the contour, the character of the inlay, the drapery in the recess, all speak the touch of a master-hand. The maker says, "The use of this piece is to accommodate a lady with conveniences for writing, reading, and holding her trinkets, and other articles of that kind. The style of finishing them is elegant, being often richly japanned, and veneered with the finest satin-wood. The manufacturing part is not very difficult, but will admit of the following remarks. The middle drawer over the knee-hole has a slider to write on, and those on each side are plain. The doors under them are hung with pin hinges, and in the inside there is one shelf in each. The cupboard within the knee-hole is fitted up in small drawers, and sometimes only a shelf.

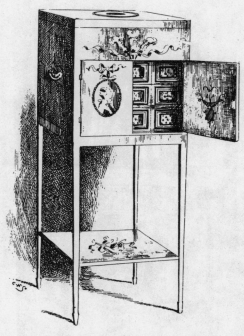

FIG. 182.—COIN-CABINET IN SATIN-WOOD, INLAID AND PAINTED IN THE SHERATON STYLE.

The pilasters, or half columns, are put on after the carcass is made. The corner ones are planed square first, and then rabbeted out to receive the angle of the carcass, and afterwards deal is glued in a slight manner into the rabbet, that it may be easily taken out after the column is turned. The centre door of the upper part is square at the top, opening under the astragal which finishes the cove part. The pilasters are on the door frame, and the drapery is formed and sewed to the silk, and both tacked into a rabbet together. Behind the silk door are sliding shelves for small books. The wings are fitted up as shown in the design on the right, or with more small drawers, having only two or three letter-holes at the top."

Some of Sheraton's designs for cabinets were too much given to mere cleverness of construction, though in this article ingenuity and utility are most happily combined.   One cabinet (Fig. 183) becomes a writing-table through the front being hinged so as to allow of its assuming a horizontal

FIG. 183.—CABINET WITH SLIDING FALL FRONT.   Sheraton.

position.   This would project beyond the table were not provision made for its slipping backwards into the lower part of the cabinet.   The top of the table, as well as the inlaid front, are preserved from injuring each other by two sliding supports, covered with green baize; which, when not in use, are concealed in the cabinet, but can be shot out by means of a spring.

The custom of using bedrooms as sitting-rooms and studies, already alluded to, gave rise to many ingenious contrivances in folding furniture. They were partly a fashion, and partly the result of want of space.   Intricate dressing-tables which closed and became unrecognisable as such, writing bureaux and desks combined with bedroom furniture, are continually to be met with.   Wash-stands which folded their wings and became cabinets were made in elaborate inlays of satin and coloured woods, thus allowing them to be seen by visitors without the original purpose being suspected.   The designing of furniture which could be used for more than one purpose appealed strongly to Sheraton, as it afforded opportunities for displaying his turn for mechanical invention, and in some cases his contrivances

FIG. 184.—DECORATED DRESSING-CHEST WITH SECRETAIRE, IN THE SHERATON STYLE.

distinctly add to the value of the furniture.   His drawing-table is so contrived that it can be used by a person either in a sitting or a standing posture, and the chief object of his lady's toilet-box is to dispense with the use of hand-mirrors.   The set of library steps made for the King is so arranged that "they take down and shut up within the table in the space of half a minute."   The table, when the steps are enclosed, serves as a library table, and has a rising flap, supported by "a horse to write on." The steps are 5 feet 5 inches from the floor, and the hand-rail at the top is 3 feet above, fitted with a small flap on which a book may rest, "so that a gentleman, when he is looking for any book, may note down a passage from it without the trouble of going down again."   Though the steps may appear

slight and rather unsafe, Sheraton proudly informs us that they were
"highly approved by the King as in every way answering the intended

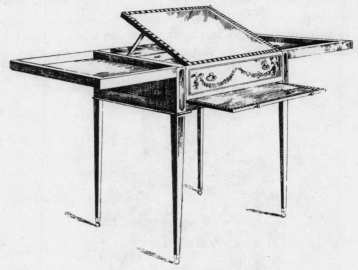

Fig. 185.—Folding Dressing-table.   Sheraton.

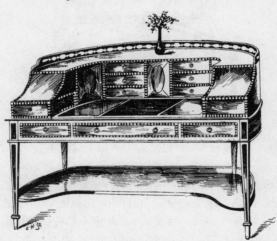

Fig. 186.—Writing and Drawing Table.   Sheraton.

purpose," and tells us that they were an improvement on those made by Mr.
Robert Campbell, Marylebone Street, Upholsterer to the Prince of Wales.
This allusion shows us how the names of many men of equally good standing

in their trade have passed into complete oblivion.   France and Elliot strike
unfamiliarly on our ears, and yet they held royal appointments, while
numbers of others equally unknown are included in the list of subscribers
to Sheraton's work.

No one can carefully study the furniture of the whole century without
being struck by the great importance attached to literary appointments.

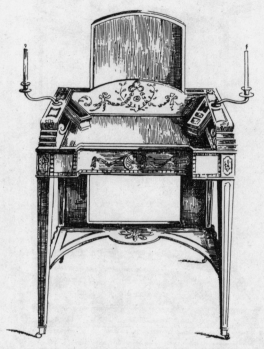

Fig. 187.—Lady's Writing-table with Sliding Fire-screen.   Sheraton.

All the fittings necessary for studies and libraries are particularly well cared
for in the various books of design.   In Chippendale, Ince and Mayhew, and
the earlier works, library tables, steps, reading-desks, and bookcases abound.
In the later Sheraton period the list is still more ample and elaborate.   But
this was a cultured century, and its years witnessed many a celebrated man
of letters, poet, and dramatist rise and pass away.   The booksellers' and
publishers' shops which these men frequented were close to where the
cabinet-makers worked, and even their places of meeting were at no great

distance. When the frequent intellectual evenings at Sir Joshua Reynolds's house developed into the "Literary Club," it held its gatherings at Gerrard Street, Soho, close to Chippendale's house and to Broad Street, Golden Square, where Ince and Mayhew, and afterwards Sheraton, carried on business. Johnson, Reynolds, Goldsmith, Burke, and Garrick were among the early members, and such men as these must have cast an influence even upon the

FIG. 188.—WRITING CABINET. Sheraton.

furniture of the period. Sheraton evidently numbered litterateurs among his customers, and not only made toilet-tables for Mrs. Siddons, but writing-cabinets suited to Mrs. Radcliffe or Mrs. Inchbald. Cylinder desks and bookcases, writing cabinets and tables, "secretaries" for ladies and gentle-men, with every convenience for keeping loose papers together and yet close to one's hand—nothing is omitted likely to assist the writer, and yet the beauty of the marquetry, the bands of inlay and delicate brass-work, are such as to recommend it equally to the man of taste. Secretaire drawers or writing contrivances of some sort are nearly always introduced into the cabinets and other furniture. Kidney writing-

FIG. 189.—KIDNEY WRITING-TABLE Sheraton.

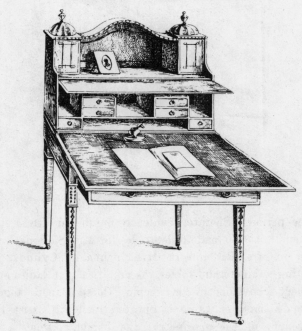

FIG. 190.—LADY'S CABINET AND WRITING-TABLE. Sheraton.

tables with adjustable bookstands are a "novelty" he provides, and large library tables with movable desks at the side were executed for the Duke of York. Sheraton's never-failing finish is illustrated in the little writing-table (Fig. 190), for the "front, enclosing the nest of drawers, when pulled out sufficiently, falls down and locks into the folding top," one fastening thus securing both. The larger library furnishings were not forgotten, for handsome bookcases were made in richly figured veneers of choice old mahogany, with marvels of cabinet-making in the shape of

FIG. 191.—DECORATED TABLE. Sheraton.

cross-banding and rounded corners. Nothing was spared which could add to their beauty—neither delicate carving, draped recesses, nor door mouldings of marvellous beauty.

Tables were another form of furniture which Sheraton thoroughly enjoyed providing: card, "universal," screen, writing, reading, dressing, and work tables form but a small number of his designs. Those known as "Pembroke," from the name of the lady who first ordered one, have exquisitely inlaid or painted ovals of figures surrounded by wreaths and drapery, and pier-tables (similar to that in our large group) are shown in his drawing-room section as well as separately. They were usually

Fig. 192.—Sheraton Table with Lacquer Panels.

Fig. 193.—Painted Pembroke Table. Sheraton.

surmounted by a mirror, and differ from those of Hepplewhite both in shape and in the stretcher rails, which are an effective addition. "These take off the long appearance of the legs, and make the under part appear more furnished, besides affording an opportunity of fixing a vase or basket of flowers, which, with the reflection of a glass behind, produce a brilliant appearance." This underframing is a familiar feature in Sheraton's work, as well as the introduction of drapery, either real or painted. Anything which would add to the completeness was seized upon by him ; and his

FIG. 194.—INLAID TABLE.   Sheraton.

cabinet doors, sofas, and work-tables are generally enriched by a drawn curtain of green silk. The fabrics employed were always carefully studied, whether they were to be used as coverings for sofas and chairs or gathered behind the lattice-work of a bookcase. "Fancifulness, which is most peculiar to the taste of females," was not altogether absent from his own mind.

Though this Master Cabinet-maker took high ground as a teacher throughout the book from which we have been quoting, his later works failed to sustain his reputation. The *Cabinet-maker's Dictionary*, published in 1803, though by no means complete as a dictionary of trade terms, gives much general information regarding the furniture in use at the beginning of the century; for Sheraton was not only thoroughly conversant with the working, but a great exponent of his craft as well. Unfortunately, the later furniture departs from the simplicity of his earlier

Fig. 195.—Bookcase from Gray House, Perth, in Sheraton's later style.

efforts, and develops a heaviness hitherto unknown in his articles. Much that he had designed previously was altered to suit his later notions, and zoological atrocities began to appear on most of the extremities. These grew more and more hideous, till, in the *Cabinet-maker, Upholsterer, and General Artist's Encyclopædia* (1804 to 1807, unfinished), they culminate in a clumsy following of the Grecian revival prevalent in France during

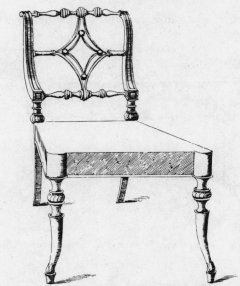

FIG. 196.—SHERATON PARLOUR CHAIR (1805).

FIG. 197.—WORK-TABLE IN SHERATON'S LATER STYLE.

the period of the Consulate and Empire.   That he felt he was forsaking

FIG. 198.—SOFA TABLE IN SHERATON'S LATER STYLE (1804).

FIG. 199.—DRAWING-ROOM CHAIR.   Sheraton (1805).

the high standard of his old work seems evident; for, when comparing a
massive Grecian bed of his own design with a much lighter one he had

previously made, he admits that the earlier production excels in beauty because of its unity and simplicity. Prompted by the rapidly deteriorating popular taste to adopt the Grecian mania, his later work exhibits all the faults of the Empire style, without the beauty of the metal mountings which partially redeems the French work.

These later chairs, cabinets, and tables are inlaid with scrolls and lines

FIG. 200.—DRAWING-ROOM CHAIR. Sheraton (1805).

of flat brass, and mounted with figures or the heads and claws of animals. One chair is "composed of a griffin's head, neck, and wing, united by a transverse tie of wood, over which is laid a drapery, thrown easily over and tacked to behind. The front consists of a dog's head and leg, with shaggy mane, joined by a reeded rail." Another drawing-room chair has "two camels' or dromedarys' heads, with a drapery thrown over their backs, the legs of which form the back feet of the chair; the front is two lions with a drapery over them also." The design in every case is heavy almost to ugliness; in fact, the deterioration which a few short years brought about is positively painful, and can only be laid down to approaching old age. While his ultra-following of French fashions led him to this exhibition of his failing powers and judgment, his fancy for brilliant decoration caused him to print the plates in colours, thereby adding intensified vulgarity and commonness to the design.

Yet it is difficult to say whether the poorness of his later work was the fault of the man or of his customers. We know that Sheraton died in what might almost be called absolute poverty, but which was cause, and which effect, it is impossible to say. The falling-off in his work may have been the reason of his reduced circumstances, while, on the other hand, the huge difference between the artistic merit of his early and his later styles suggests the despairing effort of a starving artist to catch the eye of a public whose taste was already vitiated. The greater part of his life seems to have been a struggle. In his youth he was employed as a carver in the country, where he could not have acquired much capital ; for, after he was established in business in London, Black, a member of the well known publishing firm, assisted him to bring out his first book. While at the zenith of his fame, he must have been fairly opulent, yet he himself tells us in his *Dictionary*, how, while he was "racking his invention to design fine cabinet work," he was "well content to sit on a wooden bottom chair" himself, provided he could "but have common food and raiment wherewith to pass through life in peace."

The Sheraton school of furniture is entirely founded on his first book, which deserved all the high distinction he claimed for it. Want of originality can hardly be urged against him ; for, with the whole century to copy from, he was as truly original as any of his great forerunners. Imitations of his pieces were innumerable throughout England, and were made in other workshops from his published plates. His books were reproduced in Germany, and his furniture copied there and elsewhere, but his influence was naturally still more felt in this country. "Observe breadth in the parts, shun niggling and meanness, and stick at nothing that will have a comely and pleasant appearance" was the keynote of his ideas ; and this breadth of view made itself strongly felt everywhere. Good work of any kind has always a far-reaching influence, and the direct simplicity of Sheraton's main work taught a useful lesson. The influence of his Greek monstrosities soon died out, though Thomas Hope (*Household Furniture and Interior Decorations*, 1807) and George Smith (*Book of*

One Hundred and Fifty-eight Designs, 1808, and *The Cabinet-maker's and Upholsterer's Guide*, 1826) endeavoured to keep the pseudo-classic style alive without the vulgar elements which Sheraton introduced. Brass inlay was taken up and improved on by Gillow, but after this everything worthy of the name of furniture designing ceased to exist.

One reason for this lay in the fact that all guidance as regards the interior fittings or furniture of a house was taken out of the architect's hands. The fine wood panelling and architectural mouldings had died, and even mantelpieces, the joy of the old architects, were made wholesale by men who had not the faintest suspicion of artistic taste. Wall-papers, furniture, and all inside decoration were left entirely to the unaided judgment of the householder. It was the beginning of a new era. There was no universal "oracle of taste"; each man was a law unto himself. Even where a manufacturer possessed better taste than his customers, it was impossible for him to use it. With over-competition becoming more and more pronounced every year, it was out of the question for him to think of the few. To succeed commercially, he had to study public taste; not to form it. From a teacher the producer had become a slave, and the rapid decay of the artistic was the immediate result.

Another fact is that really high class furniture design has never yet been achieved except by two classes of men, architects and actual workmen. But now we have no Adam, for the greater number of our architects think chairs and sideboards beneath their notice; nor have we a Chippendale, because our workmen's fingers are trained and their heads left alone.

The whole system has changed. Trades Unions are all very well in their way, and they have undoubtedly placed the ordinary workman in a very different position with regard to his employer than was once the case. Though the ordinary workman has thus gained by the changes brought about, the skilled workman has not. Indeed it is more true to say that, instead of his losing, we have lost him. He has practically ceased to exist. Nor is this wonderful. A man must have some motive for advancement before he will take much trouble to improve himself. Why should he burn the midnight oil qualifying himself to design his own furniture, or in learning French, so as to understand the furniture books written in that language, or in studying perspective, conic sections, or a dozen other subjects, like his predecessor of last century? All that is required, all that is paid for, one might almost say all that is allowed—is a dead level of mediocrity.   Is there any cause for surprise that everything connected with furniture has deteriorated ?   Even the wood of which the articles are made has, in too many instances, been bought by men who have no knowledge of the workshop, where alone it is possible to learn ; and if the wood is bad, the design is worse.   Happily there are a few notable exceptions, but as a rule the wood is quite good enough for either the design or the workmanship.   For the lack of the latter, we have ourselves to blame. We insist on getting things cheap, and prices have to be cut so close that every hour of extra labour tells.   But design is another matter.   We have proved by the prices we pay for the articles fashioned by the great designers of last century that we can at least appreciate design when we see it. That it is not forthcoming is because the designer is not himself a workman, and does not sufficiently understand the structural qualities necessary.

Not even the most sanguine of us can expect that the furniture of any part of the Victorian era will ever be as highly prized as that of the last century.   We are bound to admit that, as far as regards evolving a school with either individuality or great artistic merit, we do not come up to the standard of the past.   But, whatever our creative deficiencies, at least let posterity remember that this generation has rescued from almost certain destruction what remained of the productions of the Chippendale period.

INDEX

Under the names of authors complete lists of their works have been given, whether referred to in the text or not.